Jiménez de Cisneros:

On the Threshold of
Spain's Golden Age

Medieval and Renaissance Texts and Studies

Volume 212

Renaissance Masters 3

Richard J. Schoeck
General Editor

Jiménez de Cisneros:
On the Threshold of
Spain's Golden Age

by

ERIKA RUMMEL

Arizona Center for Medieval and Renaissance Studies
Tempe, Arizona
1999

A generous grant from
The Program for Cultural Cooperation Between
Spain's Ministry of Culture and United States' Universities
has assisted in meeting the publication costs of this volume.

Library of Congress Cataloging-in-Publication Data

Rummel, Erika, 1942–
     Jiménez de Cisneros : on the threshold of Spain's Golden Age / by
Erika Rummel.
          p.   cm. — (Medieval & Renaissance texts & studies; v. 212. Renais-
sance masters ; 3)
     Includes bibliographical references.
     ISBN 0-86698-254-X (alk. paper)
     1. Jimánez de Cisneros, Francisco, 1436?–1517.   2. Spain—History—
Ferdinand and Isabella, 1479–1516.   3. Statesmen—Spain—Biography.   4. Car-
dinals—Spain—Biography.   I. Title.   II. Medieval & Renaissance Texts &
Studies (Series) ; v. 212.   III. Medieval & Renaissance Texts & Studies
(Series). Renaissance masters ; 3.
DP166.X5 R86   1999
946.03—dc21   99-054901

∞
This book is made to last.
It is set in Garamond,
smythe-sewn, and printed on acid-free paper
to library specifications.

Printed in the United States of America

Table of Contents

GENEALOGICAL TABLE

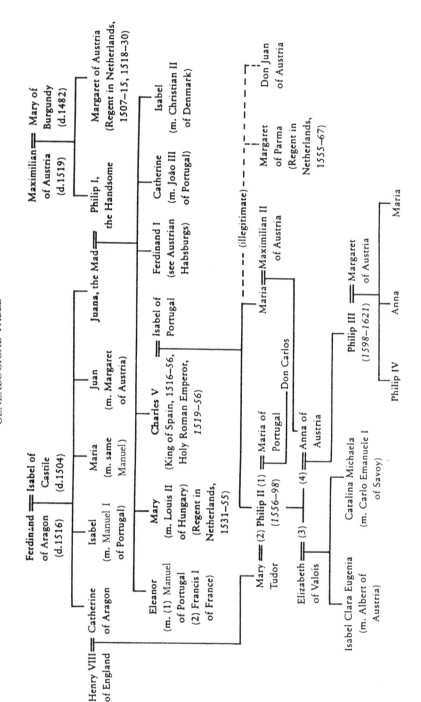

Preface

It is indicative of the dearth of English literature on Cisneros' life that a recent publication cites as "the most judicious account" a chapter in a Spanish book on Erasmus (M. Bataillon's *Erasmo y España*, Mexico 1966, cited by Bentley, p. 70). Similarly, an entry on Cisneros in a biographical dictionary (*Contemporaries of Erasmus: A Biographical Register of the Renaissance and Reformation*, Toronto 1986) lists three biographies, respectively dating from 1851 (by Hefele, written in German, available in English translation), 1914 (by Lyell, in English), and 1930 (by Fernández de Retana, in Spanish). The most recent biography in English is W. Starkie's *Grand Inquisitor: Being an Account of Cardinal Ximénez de Cisneros and His Times* (London, 1940). Clearly, there is a lack of biographies for English readers. In Spanish literature, by contrast, Cisneros has received a great deal of attention. A plethora of books and articles has appeared in the last twenty years, ranging from Cruz Martínez Esteruelas' popular paperback, *Cisneros, de presidario a rey* (Barcelona, 1992) to José García Oro's scholarly study, *El Cardenal Cisneros* (2 volumes, Madrid, 1992–93). The majority of these publications are, however, meant for specialists. García Oro's book provides an account that covers the full scope of Cisneros' activities, but it assumes a thorough knowledge of the period and is burdened with minute detail. For an undergraduate readership it is labyrinthine. Other Spanish accounts deal with specific aspects of Cisneros' career, most often related to his activities as a churchman. In an earlier work, *Cisneros y la reforma del clero español* ... (Madrid, 1971) García Oro addresses Cisneros' reform programme; P. Sainz Rodríguez treats of the same subject, with particular attention to Cisneros' inclination to mysticism, in *La siembra mística del Cardenal Cisneros y las reformas en la iglesia* (Madrid, 1979). The most recent collection of papers dedicated exclusively to Cisneros is *La hora de Cisneros*, edited by Joseph Pérez (Madrid, 1995).

Individual aspects of the Cardinal's career are also discussed in recent English literature. His foundation of the University of Alcalá and his patronage of learning are the subject of chapters in Jeremy Bentley's *Humanists and Holy Writ* (Princeton, 1983) and Basil Hall's *Humanists and Protestants, 1500–1900* (Edinburgh, 1990). His religious zeal and his missionary spirit are discussed by L. Harvey in *Islamic Spain: 1250–1500* (Chicago, 1990) and by A. Hamilton in *Heresy and Mysticism in Sixteenth-Century Spain: The alumbrados* (Toronto, 1993).

As for original sources documenting Cisneros' career, English readers are left almost without recourse. Neither the sixteenth-century biographies by Gómez and Vallejo, nor the correspondence of Cisneros and his secretaries, nor the numerous documents relating to his office as Inquisitor General and to his foundation of the University of Alcalá have been translated into English. John Olin's English version of Cisneros' preface to the Complutensian Polyglot (in *Catholic Reformation from Cardinal Ximenes to the Council of Trent, 1495–1563*, New York, 1990) and the references to Cisneros in Bartolomé de las Casas, *History of the Indies* (trans. A. Collard, New York, 1971) are notable exceptions. My book is an attempt to fill an obvious gap and provide English readers with a concise account of Cisneros' life, acquainting them with the principal aspects of his career as a statesman, reformer, missionary, and patron of learning.

The spelling of Cisneros' name needs a brief explanation. In the sources and in modern literature we find several variants. Cisneros' baptismal name was Gonzálo, which he changed to Francisco after entering the Franciscan order. His last name appears in several Spanish variants: Ximénez, Ximénes, Jiménez, or Jiménes de Cisneros. The Latin form is: Franciscus Ximenius Cisnerius. Except in quotations, which reproduce the spelling of the source, I have used the form "Jiménez de Cisneros", the choice of the majority of modern Spanish scholars.

I gratefully acknowledge the financial support of Wilfrid Laurier University, which allowed me to consult the holdings of libraries and archives in Madrid and London. I also wish to thank Prof. Jocelyn Hillgarth, who read an early draft of the manuscript and from whose advice I have greatly benefited, to the readers of MRTS, and to the copyeditor, Dr. Leslie S. B. MacCoull.

Erika Rummel
Wilfrid Laurier University

1   *Spain in the Time of Cisneros*

Cardinal Cisneros' life coincided with a dynamic period in Spanish history, the reign of Ferdinand and Isabel. The rule of the "Catholic Monarchs," as they were entitled, ushered in a golden age, a period of consolidation and expansion that saw the emergence of powerful economic and cultural forces. Modern historians regard Cisneros as one of the chief agents in this process. "There was as much of accident as of design," John Elliott writes of the emerging Spanish empire, "but in so far as it can be attributed to any particular policies, they were those of Ferdinand and of Cardinal Cisneros" (Elliott, *Spain*, 130).

Territorial Expansion

The Iberian peninsula, bordered on three sides by the sea and separated from the rest of Europe by the Pyrenees, is a well-defined geographic unit. In Roman times, it was an administrative unit as well. Conquered in the third century B.C., it was eventually incorporated into the Roman Empire as a province, called "Hispania". Medieval authors continued to refer to the peninsula by this name although it was by the thirteenth century divided into several political units: Portugal on the west coast, Castile occupying a broad swath in the centre, the Crown of Aragon on the east coast, the small kingdom of Navarre in the mountainous north, and Muslim Granada in the south.

Castile occupied by far the largest and most densely populated area, commanding four times the territory and six times the population of its nearest competitor, neighbouring Aragon. The two kingdoms were ruled by two branches of the house of Trastámara. In 1464 Henry IV of Castile, who had no legitimate heir, designated his half-sister Isabel as successor to the throne. The eighteen-year-old princess immediately became the centre of dynastic speculations. The

princes of Portugal, France, and Aragon vied for her hand. After prolonged negotiations in an atmosphere of court intrigue, she was married to Ferdinand, crown prince of Aragon. The marriage contract,
signed in 1469, united the two branches of the house and paved the
way for expansion. The dynastic marriages arranged in the next gen-
eration resulted in an association of Castile and Aragon with the
Habsburgs in Austria and Burgundy. The royal couple's grandson,
Charles V, united a vast empire in his person as Archduke of Burgundy, King of Spain, and from 1519 German Emperor. Spanish
power also extended to Italy. Sardinia and Sicily had for some time
been in the hands of the house of Aragon, and military conquest
added to these the kingdom of Naples. Portugal, also linked by marriage with the Spanish crown, was annexed by Charles' son, Philip II.

Much of the territorial expansion that took place from 1469 to
1580 under the Catholic Monarchs and their successors Charles V (as
Spanish King, Charles I) and Philip II was due to marriage politics;
the remainder was the result of military exploits. On the Spanish
peninsula itself, a successful expedition against Granada resulted in
the fall of this last Muslim enclave. The victorious campaign (1482–
92), which had the character of a crusade and was part of the historic
reconquista ("reconquest"), ended eight centuries of Muslim occupation. Soon, however, Spanish ambitions reached beyond Europe. The
exploration and aggressive colonization of the Americas made Spain
a world power. There was a sense of imperial mission and a belief in
Spanish superiority, not only over the natives in the newly discovered territories, but also over other European states. The pride and
the political aspirations of Spain are expressed by Elio Antonio Nebrija, royal historian under Ferdinand and Isabel. "Though the title
of 'Empire' belongs to Germany, real power is in the hands of the
Spanish monarchs who, masters of a large part of Italy and the
Mediterranean, carry war to Africa and send out their ships, following the course of the stars, to the isles of the Indies and the New
World" (Kamen, *Spain*, 9). Spain's political ambitions did not go
unchallenged, however, and prompted complaints that the Castilians,
in particular, thought "they alone were descended from heaven and
the rest of mankind was mud" (Elliott, *World*, 8–9). For a time, at
any rate, Spanish aggression remained unchecked. The overthrow of
the Aztecs and Incas by the *conquistadores* and the colonization of
the "Indies" relieved the pressing need at home for more land and

resources and brought enormous wealth to Spain in the form of precious metals and other commodities that were scarce in Europe.

The achievements of the Catholic Monarchs have lost some of their lustre in the eyes of modern historians, who question the ethics of colonization, the imposition of European cultural values on the native population in the Americas, and the religious intolerance and racial discrimination that led to the persecution, forcible conversion, and expulsion of Jews and Muslims at home. In their own time, however, Ferdinand and Isabel were national icons and, being associated with an era of glory in Spain, have remained heroes of popular history. As noted by the distinguished Spanish historian Ramón Menéndez Pidal, the rule of the Catholic Monarchs "represents for all Spaniards a happy golden age, remembered nostalgically as incomparable" (Menéndez Pidal, *Spain*, 402). Similarly the nineteenth-century American historian William Prescott observes that Spaniards in his day "seem willing to draw a veil over [Isabel's] errors or to excuse them by charging them to the age in which she lived" (Prescott, *Ferdinand and Isabella*, I:248n). Indeed Angel Rodríguez Sánchez, the author of the standard handbook, *Historia de España* (III:403), minimizes criticism of Ferdinand and Isabel, reducing it to a question of ideology. In weighing the merit of their policies, he says, historians tend to choose the interpretation best suited to their own intellectual leanings.

Consolidation of Authority

The authority of the monarchs, described as *poderío real absoluto*, "absolute royal power," in Isabel's will, was shored up by a number of important administrative and constitutional changes. The royal couple had inherited a loose confederation of regions with their own assemblies (*cortes*), laws, military forces, and systems of taxation. The crown's interests were represented in each region by a viceroy, often a member of the royal family, who was advised by regional councils. The monarch thus was "the sovereign of each [country] rather than king of all," as Solorzano Pereira, the seventeenth-century jurist and historian, observed (*CMH*, 322). The Catholic Kings worked toward centralizing the system of government. In many ways Spain is a textbook case for the political developments that characterize the Renaissance, illustrating the gradual substitution of the sovereign state for the feudal monarchy that dominated the Middle Ages. Although the

authority of the Spanish monarchs fluctuated and encountered sporadic aristocratic resistance, the tide ran in their favour. They consolidated their authority first of all by creating an effective system of
taxation. Once they had established a solid financial base, they no
longer needed the endorsement of the *cortes* at every step. Equally
important was the policy of administrative centralization pursued by
the monarchs. The independent spirit of municipal councils was
curbed, and their actions monitored by *corregidores*, officials appointed by the Crown. The revival and adaptation of medieval brother-
hoods (*hermandades*) did much to restore peace and order to the
countryside. Maintained by local taxes, the *hermandades* combined
the functions of a police force and a tribunal and had the power to
quell rebellion, prosecute serious crimes such as rape, murder, arson,
and robbery, and administer speedy justice. Commerce and trade
benefited from these security measures. The monarchs also tightened
control over the administration by assigning posts and magistracies
to civil servants, often drawn from the legal profession. Unlike members of the nobility, these jurists (*letrados*) had no resources of their
own and were dependent on the favour of the crown. The monarchs
increased their income significantly by revoking grants made to the
nobility, by assuming control of the wealthy military orders of
Alcántara, Calatrava, and Santiago, and using the newly acquired
power and resources to further their own mercantilist policies.

A significant characteristic of Ferdinand's and Isabel's rule was
their personal involvement in the process of government. They
supervised projects initiated by them and followed their progress
from inception to completion, ensuring the implementation of the
proposed measures. They were ever present to their subjects, an active and visible force injecting meaning into the traditional concept
of a divinely instituted monarchy.

Crown and Church

The Catholic Kings derived considerable benefit also from their
carefully negotiated relationship with the Church. Their concern was
to achieve national control over ecclesiastical appointments and
jurisdiction and effectively restrict the taxes paid to Rome. The
church in the fifteenth century was a state within a state. The privileges of the clergy were far-reaching. They were exempt from taxes
and from secular jurisdiction. The prelates of the church controlled

enormous wealth and in many cases exploited their temporal power. The church thus posed a serious challenge to the Crown's rights and prerogatives. It was a major diplomatic success when Pope Sixtus IV gave Spain a say in the appointment of prelates. In 1482 the Crown obtained the right of "supplicating" or petitioning in favour of its candidate. Another opportunity to bargain for power arose after the reconquest of Granada. In 1486 the Crown was rewarded for returning the province to the Christian fold by a papal bull granting it the right of appointing candidates to ecclesiastical office in Granada. This was also the model and precedent that shaped the Crown's role with respect to the Church in the New World. Pope Alexander VI, himself a Spaniard, formally divided the Americas between Portugal and Spain, granting them political authority over the designated areas and delegating to them the task of Christianizing the inhabitants, collecting tithes, and nominating candidates for ecclesiastical offices. These privileges were confirmed and expanded by Pope Julius II, who needed Spain's military aid against the French invaders. It is a measure of the control the Crown had achieved over the church that in 1514 it was able to pass a decree forbidding publication of any papal bull in Spain without royal approval.

Although the negotiations between the Crown and the Holy See were no doubt motivated by political and economic considerations, the interest of the monarchs was not confined to them. Isabel, in particular, was a devout Christian and solicitous for the spiritual welfare of the Church. Calls for reform had become increasingly more prominent in Europe during the fifteenth century, and in 1494 the pope gave the Catholic Kings full powers to reform the religious orders in Spain. It was a difficult task both on account of the number of monasteries involved and the entrenched nature of the abuses to be corrected. As we shall see, Cisneros emerged as one of the leaders of monastic reform. His energetic pursuit of the matter was instrumental in implementing the royal plans.

The endeavours of the monarchs to reform the church were soon extended beyond the religious orders to the secular clergy and the population at large. The Inquisition played an important role in efforts to purge the realm of unorthodox thought. The institution itself was not new, but its direction was. Medieval boards of inquisition had been subject to the authority of the local bishop, but a papal bull issued by Sixtus IV in 1478 put the monarchs at the head of the

Inquisition. Concerned at first with the enforcement of Catholic practices among converted Jews and Muslims, the *Suprema*, as the Spanish Inquisition was called, soon turned into a powerful instrument of state control. The line between political and religious spheres was blurred in a society in which religious practices dominated every aspect of life and in which a common religion to some extent substituted for political unity. The Crown was not slow to exploit the obvious advantages of the interaction between the two spheres. The Spanish Inquisition, then, became an ecclesiastical institution controlled by a secular agency. The Crown supervised the appointment of inquisitors (Cisneros among them) and ensured that the confiscated property of those condemned by the Inquisition went toward the financing of its bureaucracy. This was an unhealthy state of things, as noted in the petition of a *converso* pleading with Charles V in 1538: "Your Majesty should provide that the expenses of the Holy Office do not come from the property of the condemned because it is a repugnant thing that the inquisitors cannot eat unless they burn." Other aspects of the Inquisition were similarly questionable by today's legal standards. Denunciations, which were encouraged and indeed portrayed as a moral obligation, were not a matter of public record. The accused were not confronted with the allegations brought against them but expected to produce confessions on their own accord. Torture, a common expedient in the judicial system of the time, was applied during interrogation to elicit confessions. The stated aim was to reconcile the sinner with the church. Such reconciliations were always accompanied by a penance, which ranged from the obligation to wear garments stigmatizing the sinner to the loss of professional privileges, from confiscation of property to imprisonment and exile. Capital punishment was rare, however, given the large number of cases prosecuted.

The royal policy of enforcing religious conformity put an end to centuries of mutually profitable *convivencia*, the largely peaceful coexistence of Jews, Muslims, and Christians. Tensions between the groups had issued in pogroms before, but not on a national scale or as a national policy which produced, in 1492, an edict expelling all Jews from Spain. The short period allowed them to dispose of their goods and settle their finances added economic hardship to the injury and distress of the forced emigrants. Religious intolerance was the norm, however; freedom of conscience was relegated to the realm of

"Utopia", the fictitious state created by Thomas More. Spanish Muslims suffered a fate similar to that of the Jews. The generous terms granted them on the conquest of Granada were soon revoked and their conversion enforced. In 1502 they were given a choice in Castile between conversion or emigration, with the proviso that in the latter case male children under fifteen and girls under thirteen had to be left behind. Aragon followed suit. Modern historians differ in their interpretations of the motives behind the persecution and expulsion of religious minorities in Spain. Although the effects of their policies are universally deplored, it remains a matter of speculation whether the monarchs adopted these policies primarily because of religious concerns, or for the sake of financial profit, or from a desire to centralize the state and establish an absolute rule.

Dynastic Speculation

The marriage politics of the Catholic Monarchs and the resulting territorial gains have already been mentioned. Although the union of the Spanish Crown with the Habsburgs greatly increased the power and prestige of Spain and her rulers, the efforts of Ferdinand and Isabel at shoring up power through political marriages were not always accompanied by success. Juan, the only son of the couple, married Margaret of Burgundy, the daughter of Emperor Maximilian, but the prince died in 1497 and his wife was delivered of a stillborn child. Isabel, the oldest daughter of the Catholic Monarchs, was married to Manuel of Portugal, but died in childbirth in 1500. The child, a son, died in infancy. Manuel's subsequent marriage to Maria, Isabel's sister, produced a number of offspring, whose marriages with their Spanish cousins eventually (but only temporarily) united the two crowns. Another daughter of the Catholic Monarchs, Catherine, married Henry VIII of England, but the marriage failed to produce the hoped-for male heir and resulted in one of the most notorious divorce cases in European history. The youngest daughter Juana, whose mental instability earned her the byname "The Mad", married Philip, the son of Emperor Maximilian. After Queen Isabel's death in 1504, the succession passed to this last surviving child and her husband. Philip's untimely death in 1506, however, and the absence of Ferdinand from Spain, necessitated a period of regency by Cisneros. Recalled from Naples, Ferdinand assumed power until his grandson Charles, born in 1500 and raised in the Netherlands, would come of age. Ferdinand's own death in 1516 occasioned another brief regency by Cisneros, until the arrival in Spain of the precocious Charles, whose destiny it was to preside over European politics for the next forty years.

Foreign Affairs

The foreign policy of the Catholic Monarchs, characterized by the historian Jean-H. Mariéjol as "quite unscrupulous but ever a-droit" (Mariéjol, *Spain*, 335), was largely shaped by Ferdinand. Relations with neighbouring Portugal were friendly and the alliance was strengthened through the bonds of marriage. Relations with France were more volatile. Two Catalan counties, which had been seized by the French, were recovered through diplomatic means in 1493, when the King, Charles VIII, wished to secure the home front before invading Italy. However, the unexpectedly smooth progress of Charles' expedition and his arrival in 1495 in Naples, an Aragonese possession, renewed the conflict between the two crowns. The fate of the kingdom took many twists and turns, but in the end the French were ousted and the Spanish claim to Naples recognized. Ferdinand was confirmed in its possession by Pope Julius II in 1510.

The conquest of Moorish Granada rounded off Castilian posses-sions on the Iberian peninsula. Fear that African Muslims might en-courage a rebellion and provide military aid prompted an extension of the crusading effort into North Africa. This initiative was strongly promoted and actively supported by Cisneros and resulted in the conquest of Oran. Ferdinand was reluctant to commit troops and money to follow up on the initial successes. His policy of limited occupation was a realistic response to financial and political exigen-cies, but meant the loss of an opportunity. Failure to secure the North African coast deprived Spain of valuable strategic support in the struggle for control over the Mediterranean during the second half of the sixteenth century.

Patronage and the Arts

The cultural life of Spain flourished under the patronage of the Crown, nobility, and representatives of the church, among them Cisneros. The Spanish taste ran to lavish and intricate decoration inspired by Moorish art. A profusion of decorative elements charac-terized the "Flamboyant Gothic" of Spanish cathedrals. Plateresque or "Isabelline" relief — a common feature in the architecture of the time — was named after the Queen who sponsored the chief architect of the period, Juan Guas. The monastery of San Juan de los Reyes in Toledo and the Infantado Palace in Guadalajara are two examples of this sumptuous and decorative style. It was only toward the end of the century that art and architecture became more Italianate and began to show the features generally associated with the High Renaissance. Isabel herself continued to favour more traditional northern art. Her preference is reflected in her collection of more than 200 paintings, including works of Van der Weyden, Memling, and Bosch.

Cisneros' foundation, the University of Alcalá, was frugally designed, but shone as a centre of learning. Under his auspices one of the most significant scholarly projects of his time took shape: a critical edition of the Bible, the Complutensian Polyglot, so called after the Latin name of Alcalá. As in the rest of Europe, however, secular writings in the vernacular played an increasingly more important role. Nebrija's Spanish grammar, published in 1492, and his Spanish-Latin dictionary issued three years later, were milestones in this development. Fernando de Roja's dramatic novel *La Celestina* (1499) was the most popular work of fiction. The social criticism of the satirical *Corbacho* (printed 1498) of Alfonso Martínez and the romance of *Amadis de Gaula* composed by García Rodrígez (1508) prepared the ground for the more sophisticated literary landscape of Villalón and Cervantes. Drama and historiography flourished. Native historians like Hernando del Pulgar and Elio Antonio Nebrija and Italian emigrés like Marineo Siculo and Pietro Martire found support at the royal court since their works helped to build national pride and lent stature to the monarchy.

It is against this background of political, cultural, and economic developments that Cisneros' life and career unfolded. Spain was entering the age of the Renaissance, and Cisneros was a man for the times. Standing on the threshold of a new era, he combined in his person the old and the new. His promotion of monasticism in its pristine form, his personal asceticism, and his inclination toward mysticism reflected medieval ideals, but also savoured of the spirit of the Reformation movement, now gathering strength. Allowing himself to be drawn from a life of seclusion and meditation as a monk to an active life at the royal court, Cisneros became a Renaissance prelate: a soldier, a statesman, a leader of the church, a patron of learning. He excelled as an organizer and administrator. As a power broker, he weathered many political storms. He had a collector's curiosity, a humanist's interest in languages, a scholar's zest for disputation. He was, in a word, a Renaissance Man. Describing Cisneros as one of the key figures marking the transition of Spain from the Middle Ages to the Renaissance, Joseph Pérez remarks that he lacked none of the features of the "modern personality". "Anticipating Luther, he understood the necessity of a true reformation of church and religion. A contemporary of Erasmus, he promoted the humanities with the aim of reforming university studies. A supporter of the Catholic Monarchs, he continued their programme of building a modern state" (Pérez, *Cisneros*, 7). Cisneros' impressive career at court began as confessor to the Queen and evolved as he was appointed successively Archbishop of Toledo and Primate of Spain, Inquisitor General, and Cardinal. His career placed him at the centre of military campaigns, political intrigues, and ecclesiastical conflicts. He served as regent of Castile in times of crisis, following the death of Philip I in 1506 and that of Ferdinand in 1516. His own death coincided with the arrival in Spain of the young monarch, Charles I, bringing to an end a long career of loyal service to the Crown and a life of uncompromising zeal for the Christian faith.

Cisneros' Earliest Biographers

The earliest descriptions of the life and career of the Cardinal have the character of eulogies rather than historical accounts. They contain much anecdotal evidence of doubtful authenticity that cannot be corroborated by external evidence. The Cardinal's first biographer was his secretary and confidant, Juan de Vallejo, who left manuscript notes, published by the modern editor under the title *Memorial de la vida de Fray Francisco Jiménez de Cisneros* (Memoir of the life of Fr. Francisco Jiménez de Cisneros). The humanist Juan Vergara, another of Cisneros' secretaries, also collected documents relevant to the Cardinal's career, but died in 1557 before he could arrange the material into a coherent narrative. His papers passed to a close friend, Alvar Gómez de Castro, a native of Toledo and alumnus of Alcalá. Gómez drew on both Vallejo's and Vergara's writings, incorporating them into his effusive account of Cisneros' life in *De rebus gestis a Francisco Ximenio Cisnerio, Archiepiscopo Toletano* (The deeds of Franciscus Ximenius Cisnerius, archbishop of Toledo), published at

Alcalá in 1569. He explained the genesis of the work in his prologue:

> There [in Toledo] I had occasion to enjoy the frequent compa-
> ny of Juan Vergara, who had been made secretary to Jiménez
> on account of his knowledge and his personal worth. We often
> talked of the prudence and magnanimity of Jiménez and of his
> other virtues. In the end I kindled the enthusiasm of Vergara,
> who was already an old man and plagued by grave illnesses, so
> that he decided to write about the deeds of Jiménez. In the first
> heat of passion he gave an excellent account of the origin and
> childhood of this exemplary man. And although he wrote only
> a few pages, we owe Vergara a great debt nevertheless, for he
> diligently rescued from obscurity many little-known details that
> set the pattern for Jiménez' private life. ... But once the first
> ardour cooled, Vergara wrote nothing more during the remain-
> ing three years of his life as his health deteriorated. Not that he
> lacked the will, but the mental vigour essential to the task of
> writing evaporated as death drew near. Once this man, who was
> worthy of a longer life, had died, the University of Alcalá fi-
> nally decided to take an interest in an enterprise that promised
> such glory to the institution and its alumni, and entrusted to me
> the laborious task of writing the biography. They realized that
> my collaboration with Vergara made me as knowledgeable of
> the business as one could be, although I am in no way compara-
> ble to him. And so I received the memoirs and the other docu-
> ments which Vergara had prepared for the purpose. (24–5)

The circumstances in which Gómez composed the biography explain
why we cannot expect from the author a critical analysis of Cisneros'
actions. Commissioned by the university to commemorate its founder and relying on the memoirs of men who were devotees of the
Cardinal, Gómez was bound to give a heroic tint to his narrative and
present matters in the best possible light.

Upbringing and Education

We have no documentary evidence for the Cardinal's date of
birth, but according to his biographers, Gonzálo Jiménez de Cisneros was born in 1436 at Torrelaguna, a small town some fifty
kilometers northeast of Madrid. He was the oldest son of Alfonso
Cisneros, a receiver of tithes, and Maria de Astudillo de la Torre.

Both were descendants of well-established families. As a boy Gonzalo received instruction from an uncle, his father's brother Alvaro, a cleric who held a benefice in the vicinity of Torrelaguna. It is not clear whether he continued his education at Salamanca, where he eventually attended university, or at the *estudio general* attached to the Franciscan monastery in Alcalá.

He appears to have been a high-spirited young man, ending up behind bars on one occasion for playing his guitar late at night and disturbing the peace of his neighbours. We have little information about his academic pursuits. His biographers are vague about the courses he took and the year in which he graduated. Vallejo, in his usual hagiographic style, reports that Cisneros' parents observed the young man's talents, "his great nobility and dignity and the zealous interest he took in his studies and his commitment to excellence and service to God our Lord, and saw to it that he was sent to the University of Salamanca where ... he became a great scholar and took the degree of bachelor of law" (Vallejo, *Memorial*, 2). According to Gómez (*De rebus gestis*, 32), Cisneros also attended lectures in theology given by "Maestro Roa" who is documented at the university from 1463 to 1480. If this information is correct, it supplies us with a rough time frame for his studies. Cisneros does not appear to have held a bursary. If he was supported entirely by his family, he no doubt experienced hardships. Hunger, cold, and quartan fever were the constant companions of poor students. They were in the habit of stamping their feet in class, "for two reasons," as a contemporary explained: "to interrupt the professor [whose lectures ran overtime] and to keep their feet warm" (Retana, *Cisneros*, 1:44).

Uceda

After his graduation, Cisneros pursued a career in the church. To further his chances for promotion he travelled to Rome. His journey there and his stay in the city have been much embroidered by his biographers. We are told that Cisneros had the misfortune of falling prey to robbers twice. Left destitute, he was rescued by a former schoolmate whose generous help enabled him to reach his destination. Cisneros' biographers further tell us that his stay in Rome was interrupted by the death of his father and that he returned to the city a second time. Both claims are doubtful, however, and present chronological difficulties.

Rome was a propitious place for Spaniards in the fifteenth century. Pope Calixtus III (1455–8), a native of Valencia, had brought a Spanish retinue to Rome and raised his nephews Alexander and Rodrigo Borgia (later Pope Alexander VI) to positions of power. His nepotism — excessive even by the standards of the time — made him enemies. After his death in 1458, hostilities broke out against the pope's "Catalan" protegés, but they were not easily dislodged, and Cisneros likely benefited from the residual influence of his compatriots. Calixtus' successor, Pius II (1458–64), pursued a policy of friendship with Spain as a matter of self-interest, supporting Ferrante, the natural son of Alfonso V of Aragon, against the claims to the Neapolitan throne of the French.

Cisneros travelled to Rome some time before 1471 under Pius' successor Paul II (1464–71) and returned with an *expectativa*, a papal brief giving him title to the next vacant benefice in the diocese of Toledo. The selling of *expectativae* as a means of filling the papal coffers was a common, if illegitimate, practice. Condemned as corrupt and simoniacal, the practice was expressly forbidden by the Third Lateran Council in the twelfth century. It was too well established, however, to be suppressed at once and was eliminated only in the sixteenth century by the Council of Trent. The buyer of an *expectativa*, much like a modern investor in futures, ran a certain risk and had to be patient. When the hoped-for benefice fell vacant, he often had to defend his right against other contenders. His main difficulty was to secure endorsement by the local bishop, who was usually inclined to promote the interests of his own candidate. This was also Cisneros' experience.

When a benefice became vacant in Uceda, to which Cisneros' native town was attached, he put forward his claim. A legal wrangle ensued with Alfonso Carrillo, the archbishop of Toledo, whose privilege it was to make the appointment and who had reserved the benefice for one of his retainers. According to Cisneros' early biographers, who may have dramatized the account, he was imprisoned for a time, but swore that "having just title to the office he was not going to forfeit it; and he would die rather than obey His Lordship [the archbishop]" (Gómez, *De rebus gestis*, quoted Retana, *Cisneros*, 1:63). In the end he succeeded in his quest and became archpriest of Uceda. Here, finally, we are on solid historical ground.

A papal document, dated 3 December 1471, confirms Cisneros'

appointment (García Oro, *Cisneros*, 1:30). The brief sheds additional light on the affair. We learn that the benefice at Uceda was not vacated by death; rather the incumbent was removed because he had released a member of the clergy to the secular court. The circumstances surrounding the case are rather curious. The papal document reveals that a certain Pedro Encina, a member of the clergy who "lived in marriage with a young woman, was accused of theft. To escape the death penalty ... he sought asylum in St. Magdalene at Torrelaguna, which was in the jurisdiction of the archpriest [of Uceda, Pedro García de Guaza]." The archpriest, however, disregarded the clerical privilege of the refugee and handed him over to a secular judge, who condemned him to death and had him decapitated. The irregular conduct of the archpriest was reported to the Holy See by none other than Cisneros, who had of course a personal interest in seeing the priest prosecuted and relieved of his office. The papal document states: "The said Pedro García has shown himself unworthy of the office of archpriest which he held. ... Wishing to bestow a special favour on the aforementioned Gonzálo [Cisneros], in view of his aforesaid gifts and merits ... we relieve Pedro García of his benefice by way of judgment and confer it on Cisneros" (Retana, *Cisneros*, 1:61–2). The dubious role Cisneros played in the affair may well explain why his first biographers chose to omit the details of García's dismissal from their account and instead stressed Cisneros' heroic resistance to the archbishop.

It is uncertain whether Cisneros was ordained before his journey to Rome or during his stay there. Nor do we know whether he felt a genuine vocation for the church at this stage in his life or, like many of his contemporaries, merely chose a career that would provide him with a respectable living. His later actions at any rate reveal him as a man committed to the Church and, in the eyes of some, a religious zealot.

Sigüenza

Cisneros is documented as archpriest in the records of Uceda until 1476, when he exchanged his benefice for a first chaplaincy in Sigüenza in the diocese of Pedro González de Mendoza. It was a prudent move, coinciding with the decline of Carrillo's fortunes and political ascent of Mendoza, from whose power at court Cisneros was to benefit in later years. Cisneros' name appears repeatedly in the administrative records of Sigüenza. In 1477 and 1481, for example, he acted in lawsuits for the chapter. His organizational talents impressed the archbishop, who made him his vicar-general, that is, administrator of Sigüenza — an office that brought with it a number of privileges and benefices. In 1484, however, Cisneros abruptly relinquished his duties as vicar-general and entered the Franciscan order. It was at this time that he changed his first name to "Francisco", a common gesture that identified the bearer with the ideals of St. Francis, the founder of the order. We know little about Cisneros' motives for leaving his position at Sigüenza or his spiritual state at that time. His biographer, Juan de Vallejo, piously declares: "Inspired by the Holy Spirit, he freely left his office to a man of dignity, learning, and integrity and his benefices to other well-deserving persons, whom he thought likely to discharge their duties conscientiously, and left the world" (Vallejo, *Memorial*, 4).

Cisneros' movements over the next years are uncertain. He may have stayed at the convent of San Juan de los Reyes, recently founded by Queen Isabel. He may have spent some time at the hermitage of El Castañar and from there moved to Salceda, another rustic retreat, the spiritual heritage of Pedro de Villaneces. His administrative talents at any rate were not overlooked in the new surroundings, and he soon rose to become guardian of the house at Salceda.

Confessor of Queen Isabel

1492, the *annus mirabilis* of Spanish history, in which the "Indies" were discovered and Granada conquered, was also a significant year in Cisneros' life. On the recommendation of González de Mendoza he was chosen confessor of Queen Isabel. It seems that he had to be coaxed from his retreat. The conditions under which he reluctantly accepted the honour included the request that one or two companions from Salceda accompany him, that he be permitted to go on retreats from time to time, stay at a Franciscan hermitage of his choice, and administer the sacraments without having to obtain special permission from local church authorities (García Oro, *Cisneros*, 1:45). In his new position Cisneros wielded considerable power. His tasks involved not only guiding the conscience of the pious queen but also counselling her in her political decisions. However, Vallejo's assertion that Cisneros "initiated" the expulsion of the Jews is implausible. The royal decree of March 1492 which expelled all Jews

from the realm was obviously the culmination of an antisemitic policy that had issued in pogroms before. Cisneros' influence over the
Queen was, initially at least, primarily of a spiritual nature. Pietro
Martire, one of the royal historians, describes her as becoming
increasingly "closed off in sadness" (quoted Liss, *Isabel*, 312). The
circumstances in her own life — her age, deaths in the family, and a
sense of loss of control — predisposed her perhaps to embrace the
contemplative life that was Cisneros' own ideal. The royal historian
Marineo Siculo reported that she led the life of a nun, exerting
herself in prayer and spiritual readings. No doubt she found comfort
and inspiration in a confessor who shared her outlook.

Cisneros was fifty-six years old at the time of his appointment, a
slim, tall man of upright bearing, with well-proportioned limbs. The
eyes in his large angular face were deep-set and lively, his nose
aquiline, his voice deep and resonant. By all accounts he had an air of
great dignity. Pietro Martire, a shrewd observer of the court scene,
describes the first impression Cisneros made and the reputation that
preceded him:

> They say he is called Francisco Ximénez and lives under the
> rule and habit of Saint Francis. They report that he was at some
> time a dignitary of the Cathedral of Sigüenza, enjoying honour,
> fat rents, and great prestige among the clergy. Putting aside all
> human concerns and fearing the treacherous tides of the world
> and the snares of the devil, he abandoned it all so as not to
> become enmeshed in the pernicious desires and temptations of
> the secular world. Thus he passed from great liberty to a life of
> much constraint and to strictest solitude, not because he had
> scant means (like many people), or for lack of spirit and confi-
> dence in himself (like the majority), nor to grow plump in indo-
> lence (like others), nor for fear of being condemned for crimes
> (like certain people). They say he is industrious, full of good-
> ness, and a man of singular learning. According to reports, he
> equals Saint Augustine in wisdom, Saint Jerome in austerity of
> life, Saint Ambrose in zeal for those less fortunate than himself.
> He avoids human contact and prefers the solitude of the forests.
> He walks barefoot through the silent woods, dressed in sack-
> cloth, content with little, sleeping on straw. In private he pun-
> ishes his flesh with vigils and castigations ... A number of friars
> of his order have given testimony that on many occasions they

have seen him in a state of ecstasy, just as one reads in Saint
Paul. These and other things are said of the man. It will be a
pity if, in the usual course, the courtiers will succeed in changing his character and if some day he will become puffed up with
privilege and carried away by ambition. (Ep. 107, 19 May 1492)

When Archbishop Mendoza died in 1495 and Cisneros was designated as his successor, he was still considered an enigma by Martire:
"People say he is exceptional, not in learning, but in holiness. I have
not yet formed an impression of his true nature. So far he has not
had much contact with the court, which generally corrupts the inner
man" (Ep. 160, 11 June 1495). A few months later Martire had had
a taste of Cisneros' influence and determination. "This is the man,"
he wrote, "by whose counsel Spain is now governed. Because of his
lively intellect, his gravity and wisdom, and his holiness which sur-
passes all cenobites, hermits, and anchorites, he has such authority
with my monarchs as no one has had before" (Ep. 163, 5 August 1495).

Marineo Siculo was similarly unprepared for Cisneros' rise to
power. His *Eulogy of Spain*, presented to the monarchs in the four-
teen-nineties, contained biographical notes on leading churchmen.
Cisneros was not among them. Realizing his faux pas, he later wrote
a fawning letter to Cisneros, promising to include him in a revised
edition: "I have in mind, wisest of prelates, to add some things to my
book in praise of Spain, which I omitted when I wrote about the
affairs in Spain in summary form. I omitted them, not out of negligence or forgetfulness, but because the number of illustrious men and
deeds in Spain was so infinite that I could not include them all." He
shores up this limp excuse with further explanations. He had composed his *Eulogy* shortly after his arrival from Sicily, when he was
unfamiliar with the subject matter and pressed for time because of
teaching duties at the University of Salamanca. Now that he was
attached to the royal court he had made the acquaintance of many
more praiseworthy individuals. "And as I was contemplating whom
to commemorate first, Your Excellence came to mind before anyone
else, rightly to be preferred to them all. The sanctity of your life, the
excellence of your character, your singular learning, your fervent
love and worship of God, and your other innumerable virtues
seemed to me worthy of being celebrated in Latin so that they might
become better known in future to everyone" (Marineo Siculo, *Epistolarum libri*, 1.17).

2 Cisneros' Programme of Church Reform

Enjoying the favour of the court, Cisneros advanced rapidly. He became Provincial of the Franciscans in Castile in 1494 and was elevated to the archbishopric of Toledo on the death of Gonzáles de Mendoza in 1495. It was in these years that he began to take on an active role as reformer. Three tasks occupied his attention: the reform of the religious orders, especially that of the Franciscans; the reform of the archdiocese of Toledo; and an ambitious educational programme that culminated in the foundation of the University of Alcalá (see chapter 4).

In the nineteenth century German historians championed what is now called the "Spanish Thesis". Protagonists of the thesis noted that the Catholic reform movement was not merely a "Counter-Reformation", that is, a reaction to the rise of Protestantism. The drive to purify the church and to promote spiritual fervour preceded Luther's rise to prominence and had its roots in the fifteenth century. This reforming spirit was more particularly associated with Spain and the efforts of Cisneros. More recently, however, historians have pointed out that Italy and the Low Countries — the heartland of the *Devotio Moderna* — played an equally significant role in the early stages of religious reform. More importantly, scholars today emphasize the complexity of religious currents in early modern Europe. The ideas propagated, the practices observed, the motivation driving them, and their philosophical underpinnings are too diverse to be associated with one region or one man's initiatives. The prominent role Cisneros played as a protagonist of church reform remains uncontested, however.

The Reform of the Religious Orders: Conventuals versus Observants

One of Cisneros' first documented acts as provincial was the convocation of a chapter synod in Aguilera in 1494. According to the records, Cisneros ordered that "the old constitutions and regulations established by the founders should be observed to the letter" and that those contravening them be severely punished (*AIA* 10 [1950]: 223).

The Franciscan Order was at the time in the grip of a bitter conflict between Conventual and Observant houses. The latter preserved the rules of their founder; the former had diverged considerably from the austere regulations of St. Francis and had become feudal lords with vassals and a substantial income from rents. The friars lived a secular life, displayed the trappings of wealth, indulged in worldly pleasures, and were at liberty to inherit money and spend it as they pleased. What had originally been a movement to reform the whole order led to a division which was acknowledged by the Council of Constance in 1415. Over the next century efforts to reach a compromise failed. A final attempt at reunion at a general chapter meeting in Rome in 1506 was unsuccessful. In 1517, Pope Leo X formally separated the two groups. Paradoxically, his bull "Ite vos" is referred to as the "unity bull", because it was hoped at the time that the Conventuals would join the Observants, but it merely united the reformed splinter groups and removed the Conventuals into a separate order (Moorman, *Franciscan Order*, 585; Telechea, *La reforma*, 51-3).

In Spain the Observants enjoyed the approbation of Cisneros and the court. A considerable number of Conventual houses turned Observant, some voluntarily, others under pressure. Such tactics were not always successful, however. In a well-documented Catalan case Ferdinand tried to pressure the Conventual monastery at Calatayud into converting to Observantism. An exchange of letters in 1495 between Ferdinand and the guardian of the house, Juan Vergara, shows the latter's reluctance to accede to Ferdinand's request. A move by the King to go over his head and cite the provincial of Aragon, Pedro Castrobol, before the court, was similarly unsuccessful. The provincial refused to cooperate, and Ferdinand was forced to abandon the project for the time being.

In Castile Cisneros' attempts at reform were similarly met with resistance from those whose living standard was affected. He also encountered resistance from laymen, local grandees who had endowed chapels and feared that the necessary rites would not be performed by a reformed order. There was also opposition from Francesco Nanni, the Minister General of the Order in Rome, who agreed with the complainants that some of Cisneros' procedures were illegal. According to his biographer Gómez de Castro, he had been using every means at his disposal: "It was his goal to place the Conventual houses under the jurisdiction of the Observants by praying or paying or any other clever ruse" (*De rebus gestis*, 44).

In 1500 Francesco Nanni died and was succeeded by Giles Delfini, a man determined to reform the Conventuals but to keep the order united. His moderate stand pleased neither party. The Observants, in particular, feared for their independence. Trying to make his policy palatable, he visited Spain twice. In Castile he found Cisneros recalcitrant. In 1503 he protested the archbishop's attitude to Rome and asked that he be forced to cooperate. A planned general chapter meeting which was to resolve the issue was delayed when Pope Alexander died. The chapter finally convened under Julius II in 1506, but Delfini was too ill to plead his case. He died shortly afterwards. A papal bull forbidding the taking over of Conventual houses by Observants remained ineffectual and was ignored by Cisneros in Spain.

By the end of the fifteenth century, the Observants were in the ascendancy throughout Europe. Historians have credited Cisneros with the success of the reform movement in Spain. His determined resistance to Delfini and his unwavering pursuit of a more austere monastic ideal in the face of considerable resistance from the Spanish Conventuals earned him a conspicuous place in history among Catholic reformers.

The Poor Clares

Founded by St. Francis' disciple St. Clare, the Poor Clares (or Clarisses) were bound closely to the friars by their rule and formally associated with the Franciscan Order by Pope Gregory IX in 1227. They were founded as a mendicant order, but like the Franciscans had gradually abandoned the ideal of poverty. In the fifteenth century many convents offered a comfortable life. They attracted young noblewomen and wealthy widows, who had their own private fortune, and continued to live in the style to which they were accustomed. Few of them had the sense of vocation or spiritual commitment envisaged by St. Clare. In Spain the Catholic monarchs included the Poor Clares in their reform programme. They wrote to the Franciscan provincial of Aragon in 1497: "One of the principal issues and concerns in the reform of the convents of Santa Clara is the assignment of confessors. They should be old and godfearing and chosen only by the men who carry out visitations" (ACA Reg. 3611, fol. 143r; García Oro, *Cisneros*, 2:209). Visitations in subsequent years aimed to correct the most common abuses. They curtailed the nuns' contacts with the outside world, enforced the rules governing dress and food, and generally fostered spiritual renewal. In 1494 the monarchs put Cisneros in charge of the reforms in Castile. Cisneros pursued the matter with his customary zeal. In 1497 the convents were placed under the supervision of the Observants. Those affected by the reform turned to the papal court, but found little support.

Cisneros' examiners wrangled not only with recalcitrant convents but also with local authorities who resented their interference. Bernardino de Guaza, a canon of Toledo, complained in a report to the papal court of the indignities he suffered at the hands of Cisneros' examiners. They had "put their sickle into another man's corn ... had him taken prisoner and thrown into jail and did not scruple to detain him there. Some of these sons of iniquity, trusting in the protection of the Archbishop [Cisneros], seized the convents belonging to the Poor Clares by force, detained the nuns and are still detaining them" (García Oro, *Cisneros*, 2:222). At the general chapter meeting which took place in Rome in 1506 under the auspices of Julius II, the pope formally placed the Poor Clares under Observant control. Disputes continued in some areas. In 1512 one of Cisneros' deputies complained of the dogged resistance of the nuns at Palencia and proposed to have the rebels transferred, but on the whole the reform proceeded as planned.

Reforms in Toledo

The year 1495 brought Cisneros' elevation to the archbishopric of Toledo and the primacy of Spain, a position of great power and prestige. His appointment caused surprise, because this honour was normally bestowed on men of wealth and lineage. Cisneros had neither. The choice of the monarchs was no doubt motivated by political and economic considerations as much as by considerations for Cisneros' personal worth. Time was of the essence. A drawn-out interregnum was undesirable since it afforded local authorities an opportunity to flex their muscle and make appointments at will. Cisneros was seen by Ferdinand and Isabel as a loyal servant and a competent manager of their interests. Contemporary historians imply that financial negotiations took place. Zurita alleges that an agreement was reached that part of the episcopal income would finance royal projects. Juan Vallejo speaks of an understanding that Cisneros' personal expenses would be looked after, but that "the remainder of his income would subsidize the monarchs." They would furthermore retain control over the fortified places in his diocese (Vallejo, *Memorial*, 13). Whatever the details of the agreement, it is clear that the appointment was calculated to strengthen the Crown's position and to benefit the monarchs financially. Indeed one of the first acts of the new archbishop was the negotiation of a tithe to be collected by the Crown, a privilege granted them by the Pope in May of 1495.

The archbishop's control over appointments and funds did not go unchallenged. During the interregnum, the cathedral chapter made a concerted effort to safeguard its autonomy. They were met by equally determined efforts on the part of the monarchs to protect the episcopal authority which during a vacancy devolved on them. The chapter yielded in the face of threats and pressure, but their initial relationship with Cisneros was predictably difficult. It began with a memorandum from the archbishop expressing concern over the problem of concubinage. This was followed up with visitations, given force by a papal directive "to lead the diocese back on the straight path and recall them to the religious observance and moral rectitude to which they are in duty bound" (García Oro, *Cisneros*, 1:72). By March 1496, there were rumours of a planned insurrection, involving not only Toledo but other chapters as well. The reports alarmed the monarchs who instructed the *corregidor* of Toledo, Pedro de Castilla, to investigate the matter. He discovered that the *capellán mayor* Alfonso de Albornoz had been sent to Rome at the head of a delegation to complain — as one of the witnesses said — that the chapter "did not get along well with that archbishop, that he made them eat in the refectory and that they had to take all their orders from the said archbishop. He himself [the witness] had heard them boast ... that the chapter of Toledo had on other occasions removed one archbishop and appointed another and that this was easily accomplished" (García Oro, *Cisneros*, 1:75–6). Albornoz' initiative was cut short when the Spanish ambassador to the papal court detained the delegation in April 1496. Albornoz, according to Cisneros' biographer Gómez de Castro, spent some time in confinement. It appears, however, that the Pope was not amenable to the Spanish ambassador's request that Albornoz be removed from his post. He remained *capellán mayor*. Cisneros himself acquiesced, considering it politic to appease the chapter.

The question has been raised by historians whether Cisneros' reforms had the formal endorsement of the Holy See. Documentary evidence confirms that he acted with authorization. The monarchs had sought and obtained permission to initiate reforms. In March 1493 a brief from Alexander VI ("Exposuerunt nobis") authorized them to "appoint suitable prelates and men of holiness, conscience, and integrity," to examine, correct, and reform "some monasteries and nunneries ... whose life falls short of the requirements of the rules of their institution." They entrusted the task to Cisneros. In December 1494 the pope confirmed Cisneros' authority to reform the Poor Clares; and on December 1496, in the brief "Ut ea" (García Oro, *Reforma*, 376), he commissioned Cisneros and Diego Deza to reform the houses of the Franciscan and Dominican Orders respectively. Subsequent briefs refer to the two men as "papal commissaries for the reform" (in the brief "Ut imponatur finis" issued by Alexander VI, November 1497) and to Cisneros as "the reformer of all monasteries and houses" (in the brief "Alias ex vobis", 1501). Pope Julius II confirmed Cisneros' powers to reform the monasteries and orders and renewed the mission in a brief of 1503 (Retana, *Cisneros*, 1:129). It is certain therefore that Cisneros was acting on proper authority in initiating the reforms. However, his uncompromising attitude led a group of Conventual Franciscans to take their case to the pope and resulted in a temporary suspension of his powers. Obliging the lobbyists, Alexander wrote in 1496: "To put an end to the complaints which are brought before us continually, especially by the Minors of St. Francis, on account of the reform which we had undertaken in your realms and dominions ... it has been decreed that the reform process be stopped and the business be totally suspended until the whole truth has been found and we decide on a suitable course of action" (quoted Retana, *Cisneros*, 1:143).

Duties at court prevented Cisneros for two years after his appointment as archbishop from visiting his diocese in person. When he formally entered Toledo in 1497, his austere apparel stood in stark contrast to the sumptuous dress of the dignitaries receiving him. While they displayed their wealth, he was riding a mule, as usual, and wore sandals with straps "through which one could see his bare toes" (Vallejo, *Memorial*, 16–17). His excessive modesty was reported to the Pope, who wrote to admonish him to adopt a manner more in keeping with the dignity of God and the Church. The hierarchy in the Church, he wrote, was marked by certain external honours. "As you well know, one may sin by default just as one may sin by excess. Observing the hierarchy and order of the Church was pleasing to God. Therefore everyone, but especially the prelates, ought to be concerned, not only about their spiritual lives and character, but also about their deportment, so that they be faulted neither for proud and pompous display nor for excessive and superstitious modesty." As archbishop, the Pope continued, Cisneros "ought to observe the customary standard of dress and retinue, to cultivate an external image appropriate to [his] rank ... and the dignity of [his] office" (Retana, *Cisneros*, 1:179). Cisneros complied with the wishes of the pope and adopted an appearance appropriate to his station, but could not be persuaded to wear shoes or boots, keeping the Franciscan rule of wearing sandals.

Just as he had admonished the members of his order to return to the practices of their founder, he spoke to the canons of Toledo of the need for spiritual renewal. The speech, quoted by Gómez, although perhaps not Cisneros' exact words, reflects his general attitude. "You are aware, beloved brethren, that I was elevated to this position against my will," he said. "And no one knows better than I how unworthy I am of this honour, for I have already begun to groan under the burden and to doubt my abilities, although I trust in the goodness of the Lord and in the help you are bound to provide, giving me your support and prayers. Certainly you must help me to improve the divine service in this diocese, to reform customs, and to restore a vigorous discipline. For this purpose I wish to see in you, first of all, manifestations of splendid ecclesiastical virtue, so that you may take first place in virtue as you now take first place in honour and wealth in this diocese" (*De rebus gestis*, 672).

A good picture of Cisneros' reform programme for the secular clergy and the concern he showed for his diocese and their pastoral care emerges from the proceedings of the synods of Toledo and Talavera he called in 1497 and 1498. He asked priests to encourage their congregation to go to confession and take communion and admonished the clergy to provide spiritual leadership. Concerned about the parishioners' knowledge of the articles of faith, he instructed priests to provide doctrinal lessons for children every Sunday. In the published *Constituciones del arzobispado de Toledo* (Salamanca, 1498) he castigated parish priests for neglecting this part of their duty "so that parishioners do not know what is essential to their salvation and what constitutes the foundation of our faith, such as making the sign of the cross, saying the Our Father and Hail Mary, the Creed, the Salve Regina, and the Ten Commandments of the Church" (García Oro, *Reforma*, 337). He therefore published in the appendix of the *Constitutiones* a brief catechism to be used in the instruction of the congregation. He also admonished the parish priests to explain the gospel readings to their congregation and attached a penalty of two reales for non-compliance with this mandate. To ensure that priests were available to their parishioners, residence was enforced and failure to keep residence made subject to penalty. Cisneros also concerned himself with external expressions of respect for the Church. He emphasized that parishioners ought to be taught to cross themselves on entering the church and to turn with deference toward the place where the Eucharist was kept. The Eucharist itself and the vessel in which it was kept were to be maintained fresh and clean. Cisneros furthermore abolished the practice of charging for such services as extreme unction, to ensure that poverty did not deprive parishioners of the spiritual comfort of sacraments. Two regulations enforced by Cisneros were of administrative importance and at the same time functioned as checks on the compliance of the parish with Catholic practices: parish priests were instructed to keep a scrupulous record of baptisms and to take an annual census of parishioners who had fulfilled their Easter duty, that is, gone to confession and taken the Eucharist. The decrees of the synods manifest Cisneros' concern for the spiritual welfare of the congregation and support Wadding's assessment (Wadding, *Annales Minorum*, 1497, #8) that "he transformed the diocese to such an extent that the people seemed to have been reborn in grace."

The episcopal records document not only Cisneros' pastoral care but also his work as administrator. Here the shrewd steward of resources and protector of rights and privileges is in evidence. The case of Bernardino de Mendoza serves as an illustration of this facet. Cisneros, who had nominated Pietro Martire to the vacant archdeanery of Guadalajara, found his nomination challenged by Bernardino de Mendoza on the strength of a papal *expectativa*. One is, of course, immediately reminded of the contest involving Cisneros' own claim to the archpriesthood of Uceda. The similarity between the two cases was immediately pointed out, but the archbishop denied that the same rules applied in his and Bernardino's case. He insisted that the latter's claim had expired because the pope who had granted the *expectativa* was no longer alive. He furthermore reminded his challenger that "he had a heart of adamant and an arm of steel" (Retana, *Cisneros*, 1:271). Bernardino apparently abandoned his claim.

The archbishopric of Toledo made Cisneros a wealthy seigneur. It was one of the richest sees. While the average income of bishops was between eight and twenty thousand ducats, Toledo yielded eighty thousand ducats. The administrative records inform us that Cisneros spent about a quarter of his enormous income on household expenses, another quarter on building projects and military ventures, and half on alms. The latter went to support religious houses who in turn were expected to distribute the alms among the local poor, but sums were also allocated to specific purposes such as the support of poor students, the provision of dowries for the daughters of the poor, the support of widows and children who had been abandoned. Cisneros' record is relatively free of the crass nepotism prevalent in his time. His protegés were, on the whole, worthy men. The exception is the favour he showed to his brother Bernardino, for which he was ill compensated. Bernardino, likewise a Franciscan, joined the malcontents protesting Cisneros' reforms. His part in the plotting led to his imprisonment, but he soon obtained pardon from his brother. On one occasion a disagreement led to a violent encounter in which Bernardino throttled his brother and left him for dead. He was apprehended but through his brother's leniency escaped the death penalty customary for a crime of this magnitude. He did not reform, however. Some years after the death of Cisneros, we read that his successor transferred Bernardino to the Franciscan monastery in Torrelaguna and placed him under guard "because he does not live as he ought to" (quoted Retana, *Cisneros*, 1:199).

Cisneros continued to lead an exemplary life of work and prayer. Gómez de Castro gives us an account of the archbishop's daily routine. He arose early, sometimes before dawn. From daybreak until noon he was in his office receiving petitioners. They invariably found him pacing up and down behind his desk, Bible in hand. Unless the visitor was a member of the nobility, the archbishop conducted the interview in ambulatory fashion, terminating it as soon as possible by returning his attention to the Bible. At noon Cisneros gathered around him the household pages and personally inspected the progress they had made in their studies, ascertaining at the same time the competence of the instructors, to whom he had entrusted their education.

His meals were eaten in public and attended by a number of scholars invited to discuss subjects of interest. Among the participants in these learned conversations were the humanist Juan de Vergara, the philologists Antonio Nebrija and Pablo Coronel, and the theologians Pedro de Lerma and Nicolas de Paz. One of the guests (quoted Retana, *Cisneros*, 1:188) described the experience:

> In a twelve-months period I defended three or four theological or philosophical conclusions per day. And because the disputations offered such an admirable display of learning, many scholars attended them as well as [nobles]. ... Doctors of theology continually came forward on all sides to propose questions and ascertain the truth ... and the disputations never stopped except when the troop of soldiers stationed in the place came with their captain to present themselves before my Lord the Cardinal (for he was an aficionado of arms as much as letters and virtue), and when they had given their salute, the captain went up to the table to kiss the hands of my Lord the Cardinal, and he dismissed them graciously. Then we theologians returned to our intellectual exercises.

After lunch Cisneros returned to his office and spent the afternoon in consultation with royal councillors, conferring with them about matters of government and administration.

> When this business had been concluded, Cisneros retired to his room and for his recreation and relief from work he frequently studied passages in St. Thomas and other holy books. At six o'clock sharp we doctors of theology and his household were summoned to his study and there we spent two hours and sometimes more until dinner in intellectual pursuits, proposing questions of importance and giving our several opinions about it and attempting resolutions; and in matters pertaining to Holy

Writ, he spoke with great authority, for he was very learned and well versed in it. (ibidem)

Dinner was a frugal affair, often consisting of a sort of gruel made of bread, milk, honey, and nuts. Cisneros then retired for the night, ending his day examining his conscience and reading the breviary.

3   Crusader, Missionary, and Guardian of the Faith

In 1507 Cisneros was made Inquisitor General of Castile and acted as Inquisitor General of Aragon until 1513, when the Bishop of Tortosa, Luis Mercader, assumed the office (Pérez, *Cisneros*, 84). Cisneros' predecessor, Diego de Deza, had opposed the appointment. His letter on the subject addressed to Ferdinand was full of dire warnings: "Your Highness knows full well that this appointment would be an offense against God and mean the destruction of the Inquisition" (García Oro, *Cisneros*, 1:180). Others, by contrast, saw Cisneros as the only man capable of restoring order to a corrupt institution. Deza had resigned under a cloud. He cited old age and poor health, but other reasons had entered on his decision. He had made the political error of supporting Philip the Handsome against Ferdinand (see below, chapter 5) and his office had been compromised by the discreditable conduct of his lieutenants. The most infamous of his officials was Diego Rodríguez Lucero, who had been appointed Inquisitor of Córdoba in 1499. He instituted a reign of terror, practising fraud and extortion. Pietro Martire reported that he fabricated evidence and treated the accused with unwarranted cruelty. Lucero (nicknamed "Tenebrero") had brought trumped-up charges against young *converso* women. Although they had led, according to the testimony of their neighbours, a closely guarded life in their parents' home, they were accused of such unlikely activities as preaching Judaism and engaging in bacchanalia. Martire expressed surprise that anyone could have believed such "fairy tales or rather such infernal tales" (Ep. 385). According to another contemporary chronicler, Lucero's motive was greed and ambition. "To gain credit as a zealous minister of faith and to gain higher dignities, he began to treat the accused prisoners with extreme severity, forcing them to reveal the names of their accomplices, which resulted in denunciations against so great a number of people, both *conversos* and Old Christians, that the city [Córdoba] was scandalized and came close to rioting" (Kamen, *Spain*, 51). There was outrage when Lucero arrested Hernando de Talavera, Archbishop of Granada, a saintly man, who had treated the Moors in his diocese with leniency. Talavera was of Jewish extraction and, on the strength of a denunciation obtained from a servant under torture, was accused of judaizing and keeping a synagogue in his palace. The case was appealed to the pope, who acquitted Talavera of the charges. After Cisneros' appointment as Inquisitor General, a commission convoked at Burgos in June 1508 reviewed Lucero's activities. He was arrested and relieved of his post. His innocent victims were released from prison, penalties revoked, and reputations restored. But, as Pietro Martire commented, Lucero's conviction could not compensate them for their suffering and disgrace. He escaped punishment, moreover, through the intervention of powerful friends, and was allowed to retire to Seville.

Cisneros as Inquisitor General

The letters and memoranda documenting Cisneros' tenure as Inquisitor General show his concern for the integrity of the inquisitorial process. He inquired about the conditions of jails, dealt with accusations that fiscals (prosecutors) were embezzling the property of prisoners, and examined the nature of the evidence brought against the accused. In one case he directed officials not to imprison men on vague evidence, for example, "if they had no other suspicion or indication to go by than partial circumcision ... for there were no definite rules in such cases, and it seems to me one must proceed with discretion" (Meseguer, "Documentos," 58; the following quotations come from the same source). Among the documents relating to his tenure are numerous privileges granted to relatives of condemned persons, restoring their right to practice their profession, which a strict interpretation of the law had taken from them. Thus "Maestro Juan, physician and surgeon ... legally prohibited from holding public office by reason of being the son of a man condemned for heresy" was rehabilitated and "shall not be inconvenienced or have his peace disturbed for this reason now or ever" (100). Similarly Gonzálo Díaz of Seville was permitted to cure boils (but no other disease), although his father and uncle had been condemned for heterodoxy (106, sim.78, 79). A group of young people aged between fifteen and twenty years were acquitted of practising Jewish ceremonies because they had been under age (108). Others were shown clemency in special circumstances. A woman's jail sentence was converted because she was ill, "so that she may seek treatment and recover her health and be able to do the exercises necessary for her cure" (120). In another case, two Moriscos, who had been imprisoned by the Inquisition, had their property returned to them "because its value was insignificant and they are hard pressed" (156). Cisneros also concerned himself with procedures. A letter to officials at Toledo admonished them to attend the required meetings of the inquisitorial board. Cisneros had been informed "that some do not fulfil their duty and come to the meetings very late and are often absent, so that cases are delayed" (119). In future those guilty of lateness or absenteeism were to be fined a third of their salary. By tightly controlling new appointments, monitoring documentation, and diligently supervising the inquisitorial process Cisneros restored discipline and order to the institution.

The question of reforming the Inquisition was raised officially by the *cortes* of Monzon in 1510 and again in 1512. Agreements were signed between the Inquisition and individual provinces that put limits on the number of officials and their competency and eased regulations governing the confiscation of goods and the trade restrictions placed on *conversos*. Complaints against the Inquisition continued, however. After Ferdinand's death in 1516, Cisneros alleged that *conversos* lobbying the court of Charles, the young heir to the throne, were using bribery in an effort to obtain their goal. He noted that in Ferdinand's reign they had offered to subsidize a war against Navarre, but the King had declined the bribe, "for he wished to place devotion and observance of the Christian religion ... above whatever riches and gold there was in the world." He implored Charles "to keep before his eyes this singular and recent example of his grandfather and not allow that the court procedure of the Inquisition be changed" (Cart. Xim. 262). In particular, the practice of keeping the names of witnesses secret was vigorously defended by Cisneros. He argued that disclosure would endanger the lives of witnesses. He related the story of a convicted Judaizer, who "discovered who was the witness that had denounced him. He sought him out, confronted him in a laneway and ran him through with a lance. ... No one will come forward to denounce a person at the risk of losing his life. That spells ruin to the tribunal and leaves the divine cause without defense" (Cart. Xim. 263). The regulation remained in place. Cisneros declared himself satisfied that faults in the procedures had been corrected and abuses stopped. He envisaged no further need for reform. On the contrary, he said, "it would be sinful to introduce changes" (Cart. Xim. 261).

Not everyone shared the Cardinal's view. When King Charles held his first *cortes* in 1518, he was deluged with petitions asking him to ensure that the *Suprema* observe due process. Plans for a reform were thwarted, however, by Cisneros' successor, Adrian of Utrecht, who, like Cisneros, was content with the status quo.

The Moorish Question

One aspect of the Inquisition, the Moorish question, had already occupied Cisneros before he became Inquisitor General. In January 1492 the Spanish monarchs accepted the surrender of Granada, thus completing the *reconquista*. Arabs had invaded the Spanish peninsula in the eighth century. From the eleventh century on there were attempts to regain these territories. By the thirteenth century some advances had been made toward this goal, but eventually the pace of the *reconquista* was slackened by dynastic crises. In the fifteenth century, however, especially in the aftermath of the fall of Constantinople, the crusading spirit in Europe revived, and the *reconquista* was carried on once again under a religious banner. Six incursions into Granada in the 1450s brought few concrete results, but popular enthusiasm for the enterprise remained undiminished. The Catholic monarchs found the *reconquista* a convenient means of rallying their subjects behind the Crown. Their campaign, begun in 1482, successfully detached outlying regions until in 1489 only the central region immediately surrounding the city of Granada remained in Arab hands. The final conquest came as a result of diplomatic as much as of military activity. A feud among members of the ruling clan made Granada vulnerable and allowed the Spaniards to make separate treaties with disgruntled regional rulers. The city of Granada was besieged during the spring of 1490. In the fall of 1491, as preparations for an assault went forward and morale in the Moorish camp deteriorated, negotiations led to a surrender of the city.

The terms were liberal: there were to be no confiscations of property. The inhabitants were guaranteed freedom of religion, and local administration and government was left untouched. The new prov-

ince was ruled by a triumvirate: the royal secretary Fernando de
Zafra, the military commander Iñigo López de Mendoza, Count of
Tendilla, and the newly created Archbishop of Granada, Hernando
de Talavera. The archbishop, an enlightened man, was scrupulous in
his adherence to the terms of the treaty, hoping that conversion
could be achieved by persuasion and assimilation. It was his policy to
meet with Muslim leaders (*alfaquíes*) and to encourage the Christian
clergy to learn Arabic and convert the Muslim population by preaching and instruction. He saw to it that portions of Scripture and other
devotional works were translated into Arabic, a practice disapproved
by Cisneros who commented that he "did not want to cast pearls
before swine, that is, give up Holy Writ to those who are not yet
well confirmed in their religion to laugh at and disdain." More
broadly speaking, he was not convinced of the usefulness of vernacular translations and of giving Scripture into the hands of ordinary
people, let alone recent converts. In this he demonstrated a decidedly
conservative attitude, not at all in keeping with the character of a
"pre-reformer", the role in which he is often cast by historians.
While reform-minded contemporaries like Lefèvre d'Etaples, Erasmus, and in later years Luther promoted the idea that every Christian should be able to read the Bible, Cisneros protested that "in this
disastrous and deplorable era, in a decadent world in which the
minds of the common people have declined from the old standard of
purity prevailing in St. Paul's time, there could be no worse suggestion than to publish in the vernacular tongues the sacred words that
were to be heard only by pure and holy men" (Gómez, *De rebus
gestis*, 105).

Talavera's method yielded results only slowly, too slowly for the
monarchs, who visited Granada in 1499, accompanied by Cisneros.
The royal couple departed after four months, but Cisneros stayed on
and actively pursued the Christianization of the Moors. His interference may have been sanctioned by the royal couple, but it is not
entirely clear whether Talavera cooperated as willingly as Cisneros
claimed. The monarchs commented at any rate that they "sensed certain differences of opinion between the Archbishop of Granada and
the Archbishop of Toledo" (Ladero Quesada, *Mudéjares*, 233). While
in Granada, Cisneros focused his inquisitorial activities on the so-
called *belches*, Christians who had lived under Muslim rule and converted to their faith or had been forced to adopt Muslim customs.

Among the cases dealt with by Cisneros was that of Juan de la Palencia, who had been tortured and imprisoned until he renounced the Christian faith; the case of a man by name of Andrea, who related that he had fallen into Turkish hands in Tripoli and was obliged to live like a Muslim for five years; and that of a citizen of Granada, who asked for absolution because he had lived in the Muslim faith for about forty years, although he was born of Christian parents (García Oro, *Cisneros*, 2:510–11). Most of Cisneros' personal initiatives were missionary, however. Vallejo tells us that, like Talavera, he privately summoned the leaders of the community to persuade them to adopt the Christian faith and by their example and personal influence to facilitate the conversion of others. For their persuasion he relied on more than words; he made them splendid gifts of purple and silk garments, according to their rank. If he did not succeed in this manner, however, he used coercion. His biographers relate the cruelties committed in his name and on his orders. Vallejo (*Memorial*, 34) tells us, for example, of the treatment received by a certain Zegri Azaator, a "great noble" and man of consequence in the Muslim community. "The chaplain [Pedro Ponce de] Leon kept him for more than twenty days in chains, made him sleep at night on the floor of the prison where he was kept, made him sweep the brick floor, and physically maltreated him." Eventually the prisoner yielded to the authorities and declared "that he was willing to become a Christian because Allah had revealed to him at night that he should do so; and if His Lordship wanted everyone converted to Christianity he should commit them to that Lion [a pun on Leon] of his."

With the fervour of a zealot, Cisneros now forced mass baptisms. He reported to Pope Alexander VI in December 1499 that some three thousand Muslims had been converted. Individual baptism was not possible for such a number, and so water was sprinkled in passing over the kneeling crowd to initiate them into the Christian faith. It is also alleged that Cisneros had thousands of Arab books publicly burned, excepting only books of medicine, philosophy, and history. The Koran was in his view merely "the chief book of their superstition" (Gómez, *De rebus gestis*, 99). His precipitate actions led to a riot in the city. Three of Cisneros' deputies who had orders to arrest a young girl, allegedly a relapsed Muslim, were attacked by Muslim sympathizers, and the confrontation sparked three days of uncontrolled rioting, including an attack on Cisneros' house. Revolts on a

larger scale broke out in the Alpujarra mountains in 1500/1501, but
the lack of concerted and coordinated effort on the part of the rebels
allowed royal troops to seize control with relative ease. A more
serious revolt in the Sierra Bermeja resulted in savage battles and was
put down with greater difficulty. The royal couple was dismayed at
Cisneros' lack of diplomacy and its disastrous results. Once the
revolt was quelled, however, Cisneros regained royal favour. The
forced conversion of Moors continued. Among the few who acknowledged the attendant hypocrisy and bigotry was Pietro Martire
who commented on the mass baptisms: "There are good grounds to
suspect that they will continue living in the spirit of Mohammed. It
is of course hard to abandon the traditions of one's forefathers. I at
any rate believe that it would have been more to the point to accept
their petitions and to impose the new discipline on them gradually"
(Ep. 215).

Cisneros' legal argument was that the rebellion had nullified the
treaty of Granada and entitled the Crown to adopt coercive measures. In 1502, finally, a decree was passed, expelling all adult Moors
unwilling to convert to Christianity. The options of the exiles were
restricted, moreover, for they were prohibited from going to parts of
the North African coast. Cisneros felt that by preventing their settlement there "the country would remain forever secure, whereas if
they are on the coast or close to it and considering that they are
strong in numbers, they can do much damage, if conditions change"
(Díaz-Plaja, *Historia de España*, 24).

The Expedition of Oran

Cisneros' missionary spirit and militant fervour against the Muslims culminated in the expedition of Oran, a venture which he himself financed and organized and which carried his crusade against the
Muslims into Africa. Cisneros' efforts to organize an international
campaign and proposals to this effect made to the Kings of England
and Portugal generated warm responses but no practical help. Manuel
of Portugal replied to his invitation: "I shall with great pleasure link
my arms with those of the Catholic King and I hope that God will
bless our arms and hear the prayers of so great an archbishop, who
considers no other cause so dear to his heart as the destruction of
the sect of Mahomed," but nothing came of a cooperative venture.
Consultations concerning a joint campaign against the infidel by the

rulers of Spain, England, and France in 1507 (Bergenroth, *Letters and Papers*, #528) were similarly without issue.

Cisneros' own plan was to conduct a preliminary campaign against Mazalquivir (today Mers-el-Kebir) and Cazaza on the North African coast opposite the Spanish port of Cartagena. Once established, these garrisons would serve as bases to proceed against the nearby town of Oran. The political situation in Spain was not conducive to Cisneros' plans, however. Queen Isabel died in 1504. In her will she expressed the wish that her husband should devote himself "unremittingly to the conquest of Africa and the fight against the Muslims for the sake of faith", but he had to attend to more pressing matters. After Isabel's death the crown passed to her mentally unstable daughter Juana and her Burgundian husband Philip, leaving Ferdinand in a politically vulnerable position. The relationship between Ferdinand and the royal couple remained problematic. An agreement to rule jointly with them was abandoned. In the end he was obliged to relinquish all powers to his son-in-law. In the wake of his diplomatic defeat he left for Naples. Within days of his departure, however, Philip died and Ferdinand's presence was required once more. Until his return in 1507, a regency council under the direction of Cisneros was set up. The events of 1506/7 will concern us in more detail later.

In the circumstances Cisneros' plan for a campaign against Oran were delayed. He did, however, successfully complete the first phase. Under the leadership of Diego Fernandez de Córdoba, and the command of Ramón de Cardona, an army outfitted by Cisneros established a beachhead on the North African shore. Mazalquivir fell in December 1505, and Cazaza was taken in April 1506. It was clear that the posts could not be held indefinitely unless the grander plan of taking Oran was successful as well. Keeping the supply lines to an isolated garrison was too difficult otherwise. Sporadic Moorish attacks on foraging detachments and on the fort itself soon made an attack on Oran imperative.

In July 1508 Cisneros and Ferdinand discussed the funding of the military venture and came to an agreement. Cisneros would be appointed Capitán General of the campaign. The mayors of Mazalquivir and Cartagena would report to him for the duration of the campaign. Cisneros would bear the cost of maintaining the fleet, would be responsible for the pay of the soldiers and crew, and would finance the cost of the campaign itself. Ferdinand would provision the ships. A complex scheme was drawn up to compensate Cisneros for his expenses, primarily out of income from tithes. Conquered territory was to remain under Cisneros' administration until the debt was paid off. It was to remain under his ecclesiastical authority permanently and be attached to the diocese of Toledo. The agreement was ratified by both parties, and Pedro Navarro, Count of Oliveto, was appointed to the military command.

Cisneros personally supervised the provisioning of the army. A memorandum (García Oro, *Cisneros*, 2:542) lists the quantities of dry biscuit, barley, salt pork, cheese, fried fish, beans, salt, vinegar, oil, and water that had been supplied by the King. Cisneros' close interest in every detail of the expedition caused ill feelings between him and the military commander, who felt that the cardinal was infringing on his area of competence. Soldiers, too, commented that "the world was turned upside down": generals were praying and prelates preparing for war (Gómez, *De rebus gestis*, 259). After hectic preparations over the winter, the fleet was outfitted and ready to leave from Cartagena in February 1509. There was, however, a mutiny over pay, issuing in raucous calls of "The monk is rich, let him pay." Obliged to yield to blackmail, Cisneros had an advance paid to the soldiers. The fleet finally set sail in May and reached the coast of Africa without incident.

We have a brief account of the march on Oran by Maestro Cazalla, Bishop of Troy, who accompanied Cisneros on the expedition. The fleet set out on Wednesday, March 16, sailed through the night, and landed at Mazalquivir. Moorish troops observed the landing, but apparently did not think that the Spanish troops would be capable of beginning their operation the following day. The forced march on which the Spaniards embarked on Thursday morning therefore caught them by surprise. According to Cazalla, "the infantry was drawn up on land in four very beautiful squadrons of more than two thousand men each; the cavalry, however, could not disembark as quickly or in as organized a fashion, although they too made haste" (Cart. Xim. 243). The Cardinal and his secretary Francisco Ruiz disembarked, mounted mules, and gave orders for the infantry to engage in battle, since the enemy was now mobilizing their infantry and cavalry "and every hour more soldiers arrived, not counting the aid they expected from Tremecen [modern Tlemcen]" (244). In the ensuing engagement, the Spaniards were able to put the Moors to flight, and "our men followed them without order or direction, as each was able to run, and therefore they appeared more numerous than they were." They arrived at Oran, "took all the gates and fought in the city, especially in the mosques and certain fortified houses where they encountered resistance. Some, not content with the city, proceeded without order to the suburbs, catching up with those who were fleeing with their families and possessions. The Moors now turned on them and, because they were in disarray, inflicted some damage, but not a great deal. When that part of the city was occupied, the fleet reached the harbour and there was an exchange of fire between the city and the fleet, but finally a well-aimed shot destroyed the major cannon with which the Moors were operating, and a great many people from the ships entered the harbour. Thus they took the whole city. And before night was over, we were in full command" (244–5).

Cazalla's letter provides only a rough sketch, but is more realistic than the highly rhetorical rendition given by Cisneros' biographer, Gómez de Castro. When the battle lines had been drawn up, he writes, the archbishop — now almost seventy years old — presented himself in his ecclesiastical robes and addressed the troops. The speech cited by Gómez may not be an accurate record of what was said, but no doubt expresses Cisneros' sentiments:

> Knowing your zeal to engage in this holy war, in which both the glory of God and the welfare of our country are at stake, I wish to be a witness to your bravery and noble spirit now that the die is cast, as the proverbial phrase goes. For many years you have heard the message over and over again: The Moors are ravaging our coasts; they are dragging our children into slavery; they are disgracing our wives and daughters; they are insulting the name of Christ. For a long time now you have longed to avenge these evils and crimes ... the mothers of Spain, prostrate before the altars of God, have entreated the Most High to bless our undertaking. They are now anxious to see you return in triumph. In the eye of the mind they see us breaking the chains of their captive children, and restoring them once more to their loving arms. The longed-for day has at length arrived. Soldier, behold before you the accursed land, behold the proud enemy who insults you, and is now thirsting for your blood. Prove to the world this day, that it has not been lack of courage on your

part, but only the want of a fitting opportunity to avenge the wrongs of your country. As for myself, I wish to be the first in facing every danger; for I have come here with the resolution to conquer or to die with you, which God forbid. After all, is there a better place for the priests of God than the battle-field, where soldiers are fighting for their country and religion? (*De rebus gestis*, 279–80)

Gómez, like Cazalla, reports that Oran was taken within hours. Their accounts also agree in the description of the massacre of the inhabitants and the looting of their possessions. Cazalla writes that between four and five thousand Moors, male and female, died, and many were taken prisoner. "If the cavalry had all disembarked and followed the advancing infantry in order, all of the Arabs would have been lost and spoils of infinite value would have been taken, but even as it was, the booty taken by the soldiers is worth more than fifteen thousand ducats. ... On our side some fifteen or twenty persons died, but one could not walk in the streets of the city, which is twice as large as Guadalajara, because of the corpses and broken lances. The harbour as well and the gardens and the houses were full of corpses — you would not believe it unless you had seen it with your own eyes" (Cart. Xim. 245).

The following day Cisneros made his solemn entry into the city. One of his first acts was to release three hundred Christian captives from the prisons of the city. He obliged them to make a pilgrimage to Guadalupe in gratitude for having recovered their freedom; and indeed the chapter proceedings of that church record that in June 1509 "up to 150" came to pay their respects to the shrine. Cisneros remained in Oran to see that the bodies of the dead were buried speedily as a safeguard against epidemics. He furthermore ordered that the two mosques in the city be converted into churches. He also made provisions for two monasteries and for the establishment of a tribunal of the Inquisition to ensure that converted Jews would not use the opportunity to emigrate and renounce their new religion. It appears from Gómez' account that Cisneros was going to take a hand also in further plans but found that Navarro was unwilling "to receive orders from a monk".

Letters written by Cisneros on his return to Spain tell of his tense relationship with Pedro Navarro. Writing from Cartagena on 24 May 1509, Cisneros asked López de Ayala to combat "lies" circulating at court that he had left Oran without paying the army: "Never has an army been paid so well or provisioned so generously" (Cart. Xim. 41). Another letter, written at Alcalá on 12 June 1509, serves the same purpose. It is addressed to an unnamed "Venerable Father" at court, perhaps Juan Cazalla, and is meant to be conveyed to Ferdinand. In this letter Cisneros explains that he and Pedro Navarro "from the time when we joined up in Cartagena until now, have never seen eye to eye concerning the command" (Cart. Xim. 50). His captains behaved "like bandits, proceeding along the coast, seizing and plundering whatever came their way" (51). The two men also disagreed over the method of payment. Cisneros wanted the money paid to the soldiers directly rather than their captains "because of the fraud they usually commit" (51), but his instructions were disregarded by Navarro. The riots preceding the departure of the fleet for Oran were the result of Navarro's mismanagement of funds. Once they arrived in Africa, there were more disagreements. "[Navarro] said that it was on my account that the soldiers refused him obedience ... and if I had left matters to him and departed, he would have conquered all of Africa from there. And so you see that I did what he wanted me to do. I left him with the command and authorization he requested and the supplies for which he asked, and I gave him all the provisions in my posession, worth more than ten thousand *dobles*. All the infantry and cavalry was paid and provisioned for three months" (53).

Cazalla's account of the Oran expedition makes no mention of Navarro's lack of cooperation as a factor in Cisneros' return to Spain. He speaks instead of the archbishop's desire to ensure that supplies would reach the newly established garrison and to widen the scope of the expedition as motives that hastened his return to Spain. "All of Africa could be ours," Cazalla writes. "And that is the reason why the Cardinal our lord made such haste to return and discuss this with His Highness. ... We have heard that they tremble in Tremecen. The fear of the Moors is so great that they have fled as far as Fez. I hope that within twenty days we shall hear more good news, of other forts taken" (247). Cazalla's optimism was not quite justified by the events. Further advances on the African coast had to wait until 1510.

The winds obliged Cisneros both on crossing into Africa and returning to Spain, so that it became a common saying that Cisneros "had the wind in his sleeves" (Cart. Sec. 44–48; Cart. Xim. 245). Over the summer a number of directions were issued by the court concerning the conquered territory. Diego Fernandez de Córdoba was designated Capitán General of Oran. Cisneros' expenses were repaid in 1511 after some haggling with the royal accountants.

On his return from the campaign, Cisneros entered Alcalá in the triumphal style of ancient conquerors, preceded by Moorish captives leading camels loaded with booty destined for the king (Gómez, *De rebus gestis*, 305). For himself Cisneros had reserved Arabic manuscripts to be deposited in the library of his newly inaugurated university at Alcalá, and works of art, taken from mosques in Oran, some of which he distributed to churches in his see. To commemorate the expedition he had an inscription placed in the cathedral of Toledo which read in part:

> Franciscus Cisneros de Cisneros, Cardinal of Spain and Archbishop of Toledo, advanced from the port of Cartagena with a huge fleet equipped with troops, military equipment, and supplies. Within two days he reached Mazalquivir, arriving on the 18th day of May, and having spent the night on board ship, the army disembarked the following day and fought a battle with the enemy, whom they drove back past the city of Oran. They arrived at the gates of the city in order and using their pikes to scale the walls the first soldiers entered the city, planted the colours of the Christians on the walls, opened the gates on all sides, so that all the faithful entered together. Some four thousand enemies were slain, the city was captured within four hours. Thirty men fell on our side, by the will of God, who lives in the Trinity and reigns for ever and ever. (cf. Hefele 426)

It is difficult to assess the extent of Ferdinand's commitment to a campaign in North Africa. Pietro Martire, a well-informed source, was under the impression that "the conquest of Africa constitutes an obsession with him" (Ep. 435). Ferdinand himself declared piously that he felt impelled by God to undertake the conquest of North Africa. Indeed the *cortes* of Monzon (1510) discussed a crusade into Egypt and Jerusalem and on this occasion, too, the King declared that "the conquest of Jerusalem belongs to Us and We have the title of that kingdom" (Hillgarth, *Spanish Kingdoms*, 3:571). Such plans, however, had to be weighed against the importance of securing territory in Italy or Navarre. Ferdinand continued to support military operations against ports in North Africa after Cisneros' return to Spain, but it appears that his commitment was limited. His principal goal was the suppression of piracy in the Mediterranean, not territorial expansion. In 1510 Bugia (Bougie), Tripoli, Tenes, and Algiers were captured under Navarro's command. Navarro also defended Bougie against Barbarossa in 1515 and was willing to renew the attack on Djerba, which had eluded him in the campagin of 1510. On the whole, however, Ferdinand made no concerted effort to conquer the hinterland and was content to put garrisons into key maritime points. Cisneros, by contrast, had advocated a more ambitious campaign in the spirit of a crusade. Ferdinand's policy of limited occupation, though realistic in the circumstances, turned out to be untenable in the long run, and Spain was unable to secure real dominance over the area. More pressing problems in Europe occupied its monarchs over the next two generations, so that the territory was eventually lost.

Cisneros and the Beatas

While Cisneros was pressing for the conversion of the Moors, he was exceptionally lenient in another area traditionally subject to investigations by the Inquisition: visions and prophecies. The age was receptive to mysticism with its utopian vision of a church triumphant and the world converted by great spiritual leaders. Meditation was, moreover, the centrepiece of the Franciscan reform movement in the fifteenth century. There is also evidence that mysticism and meditation were ideas cherished by Cisneros personally. Among the monasteries devoted to meditation (*recolectorios*) was Salceda, the retreat chosen by Cisneros before he was called to attend the court. Cisneros' cousin García Jiménez de Cisneros, abbot of the monastery of Montserrat, was among the champions of mysticism and the author of *Ejercicios* based on the ideals of the *Devotio Moderna*. The Cardinal himself promoted the publication of mystical writings. He commissioned a Spanish translation of St. John Climacus' *Spiritual Ladder*, a compendium of mysticism; of the works of Catherine of Siena and Angela of Foligno; as well as of Landulf's *Meditations on the Life of Christ* and Pseudo-Dionysius' *Mystical Theology*. He also sponsored an edition of the *Treatise on Spiritual Life* of the fourteenth century mystic San Vicente Ferrer, who recommended meditation as

a means of overcoming temptations. Interestingly, however, he removed from the edition passages that cautioned readers and urged
them to exercise discretion in accepting the claims of individuals that
they had experienced ecstasy and been subject to visions.

In view of the Cardinal's inclinations, it is not surprising that he
gave his wholehearted support to the famous mystic, María de Santo
Domingo, known as La Beata de Piedrahíta. He sided with the tertiary nun in her battle for reform against the provincial of the Dominican order. Her zeal had made her *persona non grata* and the object
of an investigation by the papal nuncio Juan Ruffo. Cisneros defended her claim to divine inspiration and succeeded in having her acquitted. Her apologists, including her confessor Fray Diego de Vitoria,
described her ascetic practices, her ecstasies, and her visions. They
brushed aside accusations of moral impropriety as misinterpretations
of enthusiastic manifestations of affection. Miracles were attributed
to her: she was supposed to have answered theological questions in
trance and borne stigmata during Holy Week.

A somewhat more sceptical account is provided by Martire in a
letter to the Marquis de los Vélez in 1512 (Ep. 489):

> You may have heard talk about a certain woman from Pie-
> drahíta, who survives on an infinitesimal quantity of food. She
> has been brought to the court. The King, the Cardinal-Primate
> of Spain, and the rest of the nobility have visited her. She is the
> centre of attention. They call her La Beata. She is carried away
> by ecstasies. Her limbs become stiff, you could think her body,
> shoulders, legs, and fingers were made of wood, without nerves
> or joints, without living colour. She is stretched out stiffly, in a
> swoon, inspired in the manner recorded of the Sibyl. She ad-
> dresses Christ as if he were present as her friend and bride-
> groom; sometimes she addresses the Virgin Mother of God.
> And if she has to pass through a narrow door, she asks the Vir-
> gin to go ahead and pretends that the Virgin wants her — the
> bride of her son — to go first. Then the little Beata says in the
> hearing of everyone that she could not be the bride of Christ if
> "you, Virgin Mary, had not borne him for me, therefore you
> must go first." With these and other conversations (I was about
> to say, nonsense) of this sort, she has the court mesmerized.
> Then she speaks familiarly with Christ, and appears to dwell
> with him as his bride, whereas those who are in her presence

see nothing. The Cardinal, who is the Inquisitor General, and others who have this responsibility, have examined her and seem to approve of what she does. Thus she was acquitted and let go. Many Dominicans (to whose institution she belongs and whose habit she is wearing) have decried this; others follow the Beata and praise her holy life to the stars. They are bitterly divided over this matter. On one side they call for an end to this superstition; on the other they argue in her support. Their disagreement amuses the people. The authority of King and Cardinal, who have examined the woman's character and have refused to condemn her, increases the number of her followers who believe that she is divinely inspired.

Many of her followers asked the Beata to wear articles belonging to them to share in her inspiration. The Cardinal himself requested that she wear a Franciscan scapular on his behalf. What may have endeared her particularly to him was her vision of his success at Oran. "At the time when the Lord Cardinal Archbishop of Toledo was in Africa and at the head of the army," her confessor reported, "this handmaiden of God saw the image of Christ crucified among the army and prophesied many things" (García Oro, *Cisneros*, 1:245, n. 142).

Similar prophecies were supposedly made by another beata who enjoyed Cisneros' support, Marta de la Cruz, also of Toledo. She, however, "made a solemn vow not to tell him until [what she had seen in a vision] had happened" (García Oro, *Cisneros*, 1:249). She corresponded with Cisneros during the years 1511–12 and shared with him her views, or rather visions, about the political developments in Italy and assured him of her prayers. Cisneros also corresponded with Santa Juana de la Cruz, a tertiary Franciscan from Cubas. Because of the Cardinal's connection with her, the superior of the Franciscan monastery of Ocaña felt it his duty to report to him that the beata had received a proposition from one of his monks, who "in his prayers had received a command from God to impregnate her with a son, a saint". Apparently incarceration made the monk see the error of his ways (García Oro, *Cisneros*, 1:255).

Some mystics promoted the idea of a crusade that would transfer the papacy to Jerusalem and initiate a reform of the world. María de Santo Domingo in particular saw Cisneros in the role of the reforming pope. Similarly, the French philosopher Charles de Bovelles, a disciple of Lefèvre and like him inclined to mysticism, was made

welcome by the Cardinal in 1506. He predicted a reconquest of the
Holy Land within twelve years and the imminent conversion of the
world to Christianity. After Cisneros' victory at Oran he encouraged
him to extend his crusade to Jerusalem. Another visionary in Cisneros' circle was Fray Melchor, a wandering spirit who, disappointed
with regular orders, had turned for inspiration to the beatas María
de Santo Domingo and Marta de la Cruz. He too foretold the conversion of the Moors within a twelve-year period. Protected during
Cisneros' lifetime by the Cardinal's solid belief in their prophetic
powers and the patronage of the court, these visionaries escaped the
scrutiny of the Inquisition. Soon after the Cardinal's death, however,
their claims to divine inspiration were probed and in some cases
revealed as fraud, in others ascribed to diabolical influences and thus
subjected to the due process of ecclesiastical laws. Many of the mystical tracts, moreover, that were published with the approval and support of Cisneros ended up on the Index of Prohibited Books.

Cisneros and the Missions in the New World

Cisneros' missionary zeal led him to take an active interest in the
Christianization of the indigenous population in the Americas. His
first involvement was through his secretary and confidant, Francisco
Ruiz, who joined a group of Franciscans leaving for Española in July
1500. In 1493 the Observant Franciscans had been holding a chapter
meeting at Florenzac in southern France, when they heard of Colum-
bus' return from his first voyage and his report to the court, then at
Barcelona. The news of the discovery of a "new world" was greeted
with missionary enthusiasm by the friars, as Nicolas Glassberger, the
Franciscan chronicler, reported (García Oro, *Cisneros*, 2:598–9; cf.
Tibesar, "Franciscan Province," 378):

> [In 1493] certain experienced merchants and sailors, with the
> financial support of the King, and after great and serious diffi-
> culties and risks, discovered in the most remote parts of the
> ocean verging toward India certain new islands inhabited by
> barbarian tribes, as naked as animals and completely ignorant of
> the Christian faith. When these news came to the notice of cer-
> tain mature and zealous Brothers of our Observant Order in the
> Province of France, they were incensed like an elephant who
> has seen blood, and they were moved to seek an interview with
> the Vicar General, Olivier Maillard, who had just concluded the

general ultramontane chapter meeting in Florenzac and to ask him for permission to sail to the new lands, for they were eager to give witness as martyrs. The lay brothers Juan de La Deule and Juan Cosin, two men in excellent health and disposed to suffer for God anything required of them [were chosen]. ... They knew that a fleet was departing for the newly discovered lands. They offered to accompany the sailors, who received them gladly, when they saw that they were of good health, honest and devout, for they thought they would be a great help during the voyage, both because of their bodily strength and their spiritual fervour.

When they arrived at the new islands, they encountered a problem: They did not know the language of the people. However, they persevered in their work for five years with great difficulty and finally succeeded in learning to speak the language of those tribes. In the meantime the clothes they had brought were beginning to rot. One of them therefore undertook to spin silk and make tunics or habits so that they would not have to go around naked. After five years of work, when they saw that the natives were well disposed to accepting the Catholic faith, they decided to turn to Spain in search of priests, for they themselves were lay brothers.

The two Franciscans accordingly returned to Spain in 1500. Among their recruits were three associates of Cisneros, Juan de Trastierra, Juan de Robles, and his confidant and mayordomo, Francisco Ruiz. In October 1500 Deule and Robles informed Cisneros of the success of the new mission, but reported — not surprisingly — that the new recruits were prostrated with heat. A memorandum to Cisneros, probably authored by Trastierra, describes the objectives of the mission and asks for Cisneros' help in reaching them. There was a need for financial support and for priests, the author of the memorandum wrote. He also suggested the creation of a bishop to whose spiritual care the islanders could be entrusted. Concubinage between Spaniards and native women received special attention in the memorandum, particularly the cases of married men with families in Spain who had fathered children in the colonies. Ruiz, too, wrote a number of letters to the Cardinal. Both Ruiz and Trastierra had an opportunity to follow up on their reports in person, Ruiz in 1503 when an illness forced him to return and Trastierra in 1504 when he came to

Spain to lobby for an enlarged mission. As a result of Trastierra's representations and Cisneros' efforts, it was decided at the general chapter of Laval (1505) to establish a separate province in Española. It was named the Franciscan Observant Province of the Holy Cross of the Indies. There is evidence that Juan de Trastierra himself was the first vicar general, followed by Alonso de Espinar and Pablo de Solis. Their successor, Pedro Mexía, regarded himself a disciple of Cisneros and received the Cardinal's personal support when he requested that more friars be sent to Española (García Oro, *Cisneros*, 2:660). Cisneros was no doubt also behind the generous material support given by the Crown to the next group of missionaries setting out for Española. The establishment of a school, a project fostered by Espinar and Mexía, also had Cisneros' approval and support. In the fifteen-twenties, however, the new province began to decline, as a considerable number of missionaries left Española for new colonies on the mainland. In spite of Mexía's efforts to revive the province, the trend proved irreversible, and by 1559 the island had lost its status as a province.

The Franciscans became involved in the discussion over native rights in 1512, when a dispute broke out between the colonists on Española and newly arrived Dominican missionaries. The vicar of a recently founded Dominican monastery, Antonio Montesinos, a powerful speaker, vigorously attacked the treatment of natives by the colonists. As a result hearings were held in Spain, in which Montesinos was the complainant and the Franciscan provincial Espinar represented the views of the colonists. For this he earned the contempt of the "Apostle of the Indies", Bartolomé de las Casas, who accused him of "furthering the cause of servitude." He left it open whether the provincial was naive or truckling to the interests of the colonists. In any case, he noted sarcastically, the court treated Espinar "like a canonized saint" (*History of the Indies*, III.5).

Royal directives concerning the treatment of the native population had gone out to individual colonies on Queen Isabel's initiative, but her provisions, designed to give a measure of protection to indigenous workers, were rarely enforced. The Laws of Burgos (1512/13) constituted a first effort at drawing up general regulations governing the social and political relationship between conquerors and conquered. They rested on the assumption of the cultural superiority of Europeans and their right to impose control, by force if necessary, on a people perceived as morally inferior. The laws were only moderately successful as an instrument of curtailing existing abuses or protecting the indigenous population from ruthless exploitation by colonists. The system of *encomiendas*, which had institutionalized forced labour, was economically profitable to those in control and therefore not easily modified, let alone abolished.

Bartolomé de Las Casas

Not everyone in Spain or in the Indies shared the views embodied in the Laws of Burgos which stamped the indigenous population as "idle and vicious." They found an eloquent spokesman in the Dominican Bartolomé de las Casas, who came to the Spain in 1516 to present their case to King Ferdinand.

Las Casas, the son of a merchant from Seville, had gone to the Indies in 1502 to take part in the family business of farming and trading. He became the owner of two *encomiendas*, instructing the Indians entrusted to him in the Catholic faith, as stipulated by the charter, and treating them humanely. However, he could not fail to observe the cruelty of other settlers. In 1506 he travelled to Rome and entered the priesthood. After his return to the Indies, he came under the influence of Antonio de Montesinos. The sermons of the Dominican preacher are quoted in Las Casas' *History of the Indies*:

> By what right or justice do you hold these Indians in such a cruel and horrible servitude? On what authority have you waged such detestable wars against these peoples, who dwelt quietly and peacefully on their own lands? ... Why do you keep them so oppressed and exhausted, without giving them enough to eat or curing them of the sicknesses they incur from the excessive labour you give them, and they die, or rather you kill them, in order to extract and acquire gold every day? And what care do you take that they should be instructed in religion, so that they may know their God and creator, may be baptized, may hear Mass, and may keep Sundays and feast days? Are they not men? Do they not have rational souls? (*Witness*, 67)

Responding to Montesinos' appeal, Las Casas divested himself of his *encomiendas*, and began a vigorous campaign against the institution. In his *History of the Indies* (II.13) he also reflected on the activity of the Franciscans in Española. In his opinion, no more thought was given to the Indians than if they had been "sticks or stones, cats or dogs". And that was the attitude not only of the governor himself and the colonists to whom the Indians were committed, but even of the Franciscans "who were good people," Las Casas conceded, but who did nothing about this matter and had no aspirations other than "to live a life of devotion in [the governor's] house in the city and in another which they built in La Vega." He admitted, however, that they lived exemplary lives and may have impressed the native population in this indirect but no less effective manner. "They asked permission to have with them the sons of some caciques (few of them, to be sure), perhaps four, whom they taught to read and write. Beyond that I do not know what they learned from them in matters of Christian doctrine and good habits, other than by good example, for they were good men and lived a good life" (ibid.).

In 1515 Las Casas travelled to Spain and sought an audience with King Ferdinand, lobbying for stronger legislation to protect the Indians. According to his own account, he "made known to him the destruction of these lands and the violent deaths of their native peoples; how the Spaniards, by their avarice, were killing them, how all were perishing without faith and without sacraments, and that if His Highness did not assist shortly with a remedy, all the lands would soon become wilderness" (*Witness*, 80). His endeavours were blocked, however, by the royal secretary Lope Conchillos and the Bishop of Burgos, Juan Rodríguez de Fonseca, who was in charge of affairs in the Indies. Both were *encomenderos* and had reason to prevent Las Casas from gaining the King's ear. Conchillos tried to bribe him to withdraw; the bishop ridiculed his concerns. "Behold, what a witty fool!" he said, according to Las Casas, when told of the sufferings of the Indians. "What is that to me, and what is that to the King?" (*Witness*, 82). Las Casas was not deterred, however, and, after Ferdinand's death in January 1516, took his case to Cisneros, then regent of Castile, and to Charles' representative, Adrian of Utrecht. He addressed memoranda to them, in which he described the impact of the harsh working conditions in mines on the health and welfare of the workers, many of them children. At a subsequent meeting with the regent, he noted that the Laws of Burgos were not observed and, to make his point, asked that they be read aloud. He describes the encounter:

A servant and official of Secretary Conchillos read the laws. And when he arrived at the law ordering Indians who worked on estates or farms to be given a pound of meat every eight days or on feast days, he wanted to conceal that, perhaps because it affected him or his friends, and he read it in a different way from the way it was written. But [Las Casas] who had studied it carefully and knew it by heart, said at once there in the presence of all: "That law doesn't say any such thing." The cardinal ordered the reader to go back and read it again. He read it in the same way. [Las Casas] said: "That law doesn't say any such thing." The cardinal, as if angry at the cleric and supporting the reader said: "Be quiet, or consider what you are saying." [Las Casas] replied: "May your most reverend lordship order my head struck off if what notary so-and-so recites is truly what that law says."

Cisneros then took the book from the reader's hands and confirmed the truth of Las Casas' protestations. As a result, he ordered an investigation, delegating the task jointly to Las Casas, Montesinos, and the jurist Lópes de Palacios Rubios. Their submission, which recommended the elimination of *encomiendas* and an end to forced labour, was accepted in principle and Las Casas entrusted with its execution. In this task he was to be aided by three members of the Jeronimite order: Alonso de Santo Domingo, prior of San Juan de Ortega near Burgos, Luis de Figueroa, prior of the monastery La Mejorada, and Bernaldino de Manzanedo, prior of Monta-Marta near Zamora. In September 1516, Cisneros and Adrian signed papers giving Las Casas authority "to reform the Indies and advise other people in charge of the same task about the freedom, good treatment, the spiritual and physical health of the Indians." The document granted Las Casas "full powers, including contingencies, dependencies, emergencies, annexations and associations attendant thereon" and appointed him "procurator and universal protector of all Indians in the Indies, with a salary of 100 gold pesos per year" (*History of the Indies*, III.90).

Cisneros reported on his initiative to King Charles. "Concerning the Indies," he wrote to Brussels, "I was informed about the bad government prevailing there, and about the aggravations and maltreatment the Indians have received. I have therefore agreed to send there certain religious from the Order of St. Jerome, who are persons of prudence and complete devotion. I have given them certain instruc-

tions to examine matters and make provisions, as necessary to the service of God and Your Highnesses" (Cart. Xim. 188). The instructions to the Jeronimites had a general preamble outlining their powers which were followed by a detailed and specific list of measures to be taken. They were to "investigate the situation by requesting information, under oath if necessary, from the settlers and other sources; to study the means by which to preserve the natives and the land; ... to stop oppression, punish wrongdoers, and see to it that from now on Indians are treated as the Christian free men they are in reality. Therefore, the caciques must inform their people and hold meetings discussing what should be done to remedy their situation, and solutions found amenable to both Indians and Spaniards will be taken into account ... When the Fathers report their findings to the Indian population, they must be accompanied by religious men known to those Indians as trustworthy people in order to win their confidence and interpret their language" (*History of the Indies*, III.88).

Las Casas envisaged the establishment of Indian communities that would fully provide for their own welfare. In spite of its utopian cast, however, his grand plan perpetuated Spanish control. The villages, although headed by their native caciques, were to be supervised by a Spanish administrator whose task it was to "cooperate with the priest to see that Indians dress properly, sleep in beds, take care of their tools and are satisfied with their wives. A husband should not abandon his wife and the wife must be chaste" (ibid.). It was hoped that even the ranks of caciques would eventually be filled by Spaniards. They were encouraged to marry the daughters of Indian caciques, so that they might "become the town cacique and enjoy the same rights and privileges as other caciques. This way, it is hoped that all caciques will soon be Spaniards" (ibid.). Nor was the concept of forced labour entirely abandoned, although the workers were now assured a share of the profit: "Men between the ages of 20 and 50 will be forced to work in the mines in three shifts, rotating every two months or whatever period of time the cacique shall establish. When an individual is sick or kept away from work, he will be replaced by another from another shift. They will leave for work at about sunrise, take three hours for mealtime at home, and will return to work until sunset. No woman shall be forced to go to the mines unless she so wishes, in which case she is to be counted as a man in the making up of a shift ... When not working in the mines, Indians

will work their own land within sight of the priest or the administrator ... Indians must work their land when not on their shifts and be helped in this by women and children" (ibid.).

Cisneros also wished to see the justice system reformed. For this purpose he appointed the jurist Alonso Zuazo, a competent and principled man, but his departure was delayed for some time by those who stood to lose from his investigation. In the end Cisneros himself intervened to expedite his mission. According to Las Casas, he summoned the responsible individuals, "asking them to produce the documents [authorizing Zuazo] and sign them on the spot, which they did, making their signatures in such a way as to be able to prove to the King that they had done this against their will. Thus Zuazo now had official authority, much to the sorrow of those who had private interests in the Indies" (*History of the Indies*, III.90).

Las Casas and the Jeronimite commissioners departed for the Indies in December 1516; Zuazo followed in April 1517. Official correspondence between Cisneros and the Casa de Contratación show that he was concerned with the financial and administrative details facilitating their mission (Cedillo, *Cisneros*, 290–1). He furthermore sent out fourteen Franciscan missionaries, asking that they stay in contact with the Jeronimites and rely on their support. His office was also petitioned by individuals seeking redress in cases involving grants of indigenous labourers, but these were referred to the Jeronimite commissioners. Their efforts to implement the measures listed in their authorization was naturally met with hostility and determined resistance. Ironically the commissioners suggested that black slaves be imported to supplant indigenous labour, an idea to which Cisneros objected. After Cisneros' death, however, they successfully petitioned Charles for a licence to import African slaves into Española, because the number of indigenous workers was insufficient to sustain the colonists' efforts. The Jeronimites, then, were swayed by considerations for the interests of the colonists, and the idealistic plans of Las Casas remained largely unimplemented. In 1519/1520, finally, their mandate was ended. On Charles' orders, the commissioners returned to Spain. Zuazo's mission was similarly terminated.

4 The University of Alcalá and the Complutensian Polyglot

The foundation of the university of Alcalá, more than any other enterprise, establishes Cisneros' credentials as a figure of the Renaissance. The will to sponsor a cultural institution of this magnitude speaks of the Archbishop's commitment to learning. The financial and organizational difficulties surrounding the building project itself and the efforts to secure official status for the institution further attest to Cisneros' cultural concerns. It is his support for language studies, however, that give Alcalá a place in the history of humanism. Although it is perhaps an exaggeration to speak of the *homo complutensis*, the "Alcalá scholar", as a unique type representing Spanish Renaissance humanism (Andres, *Teología española*, 40), the significance of the university is undisputed. The focus on language studies and the philological approach to biblical scholarship practised at Alcalà were innovative and, at the time, regarded as controversial. In conservative circles the application of philological principles to an inspired text met with indignation. The first biblical humanists — Lorenzo Valla in Italy, Jacques Lefèvre in France, and Desiderius Erasmus in the Low Countries — were targets of numerous polemics. Cisneros, by contrast, welcomed humanists at his university and supported their philological and textual researches. He did, however, retain a measure of control over the publication of their findings, as we shall presently see.

The College of San Ildefonso, where the three biblical languages, Hebrew, Greek, and Latin, were taught, was the heart of the new university (a separate Collegium Trilingue was built after the Cardinal's death, in 1528). Alcalá has been compared with similar foundations providing for instruction in the biblical languages at Louvain and Paris. There are, however, significant differences in institutional character between Alcalá and the North European foundations. The Collegium Trilingue at Louvain, privately financed out of the legacy

of Jérôme de Busleiden, and the college founded under the patronage of the French King Francis I (eventually named Collège royal, and known from the nineteenth century on as Collège de France), were institutions run parallel to or separate from the old-established universities at Louvain and Paris. The lecturers found themselves in competition, and at times in conflict, with the Faculties of Theology at those universities. At Alcalá instruction in the three languages was an integral part of the university curriculum (Ezquerra, "Le modèle," 232). A harmonious relationship normally prevailed between the holders of the chairs in Hebrew, Greek, and Latin and other faculty members. The focus at Alcalá was on the training of clerics, and it was for this purpose primarily that the biblical languages were taught. According to the constitution, language studies "must be the principal object of theologians," for it was through Hebrew, Greek, and Latin that God's Word was disseminated (de la Torre, "Universidad de Alcalá," 51). While the Faculties of Theology at Paris and Louvain rejected the idea that language studies were a necessary prerequisite for theological studies, Cisneros was convinced of their merit and gave them a central place in the curriculum.

The foundation of the university was not only an act of cultural patronage but can also be seen as an extension of Cisneros' programme of religious reform and his quest for a better-educated clergy. A papal bull of 1497 ("Inter caetera") commissioned Cisneros and the inquisitor Diego de Deza to undertake visitations of academies (*estudios generales*) and universities. The papal brief makes specific mention of Salamanca and Valladolid, but more generally directs the two men to visit whatever other academies and universities might be in need of reform, empowers them "to correct and change their statutes and regulations" and envisages the foundation of new institutions (*Archivum Secretum Vaticanum*, Reg. Vat. 873, fol. 446 verso). Conditions at Valladolid and Salamanca were accordingly scrutinized in 1500 and 1501. Cisneros furthermore made plans for two new universities in Seville and in Alcalá. Only the second project was realized during his lifetime. Predictably, Cisneros' design met with resistance from the old-established University of Salamanca, which feared competition, but his plans had the support of the Crown. Cisneros persuaded the royal couple to assume patronage and to sponsor his foundation with an annual subvention, guaranteeing its autonomy.

Alcalá, the ancient Roman Complutum, obtained its modern name under its Muslim rulers. Al-Qul'aya, "the little castle", was recaptured in 1114 by the Spaniards under King Alfonso VI and attached to the archbishopric of Toledo. An *Estudio General* was established in the city in 1293, and in 1479 St. Justus and Pastor became its collegiate church. A first step toward raising the *estudio general* in Alcalá to the level of a university was taken by Archbishop Alfonso Carillo, who approached Pope Innocent VIII and in 1487 obtained his approval for a foundation in Alcalá that would consist not only of a faculty of Arts, but also have chairs in theology and canon law. The following year the pope approved the necessary benefices for the support of professors (García Oro, *Cisneros*, 2:258). Cisneros revived the project and obtained another privilege from Pope Alexander in 1499. He had, however, more ambitious plans and applied furthermore for permission to establish a "doctoral church", that is, one whose canons all had doctorates and taught at the university — an honour to be shared only with Louvain. This privilege, however, was granted only after his death in a papal bull of 1519.

Cisneros began assembling properties earmarked in the accounts "for the construction of a college" (Meseguer, "Documentos," 36–7) in the mid-nineties. In 1498 he made the protonotary Alfonso de Herrera his agent in Rome and set in motion the process of arranging the necessary finances, linking benefices with university posts, and obtaining the privilege of conferring academic degrees. The cornerstone for the first building, the College of San Ildefonso, was laid in the spring of 1499 by Cisneros himself, who blessed the structure and placed into the foundation commemorative gold and silver coins. The plans for the university had been drawn up by the celebrated Spanish architect Pedro Gumiel. He faced technical difficulties as the designated place was low-lying and had to be drained. In spite of Gumiel's measures and renewed efforts in the 1530s to sanitize the town, the site remained a breeding ground for malaria. The architect had instructions to sacrifice beauty to efficiency, and tradition has it that King Ferdinand, on a visit to Alcalá, commented on the utilitarian brick buildings, chaffing the archbishop that the structure did not seem "very durable for an institution which you want to be eternal." Cisneros is said to have answered complacently that he would leave it to future generations to "dress in marble and stone what I have built in brick" (Quintano, *Historia*, 144). Construction proceeded over the next years and Cisneros himself resided in the city as often as health and government business permitted.

The major college was that of San Ildefonso, named after the patron saint of Toledo. In addition there were seven minor colleges and a hospice for poor students. Several monastic orders also established houses of their own to give their young religious an opportunity of studying at Alcalá. There was, moreover, a residence for young women, attached to San Juan de la Penitencia. The "Colegio para doncellas," as Gómez calls it, offered instruction to daughters of poor families. Although the institution has been touted by some scholars as "revolutionary" and a significant step in the history of the education of women, there is no hard evidence that the pupils received any training beyond basic instruction in reading and writing and in the traditional skills of sewing, weaving, and other household tasks (Escandell Bonet, *Estudios Cisnerianos*, 206–16).

The new university opened its doors in 1508 with five hundred new students and seven professors from Salamanca, a university with which it was soon engaged in active competition. By 1509 it was fully operational. The academic community expanded rapidly. A number of lecturers were recruited, or rather repatriated, from Paris. Sources from the sixteenth century differ on the number of chairs founded by Cisneros, listing between 42 and 48. The twelve chairs mentioned by his biographer Gómez de Castro are the most notable ones. He lists the following subjects: theology, logic and philosophy, medicine, Greek, Hebrew, rhetoric, and canon law. The constitution of the university (article 45) firmly established the hierarchy of disciplines: "Theology uses the remaining arts and sciences as handmaids." While the hierarchy was traditional, the theological programme was not. Cisneros added a chair in Scotism to the traditional chairs in Thomism and Nominalism. It was the first Scotist chair in Spain. No doubt Cisneros, being a Franciscan, wanted to honour the Franciscan doctor, Duns Scotus, whose teachings were well established in Northern Europe. The innovation caused the university of Salamanca some alarm, but eventually resulted in its following suit. The constitutions of the university specifically prohibited the teaching of "sophisms" and "calculations", but logic and science continued to be taught side by side with language studies.

Cisneros continued to take an active interest in the operations of his university. From time to time he deposited in the university books and articles of museal interest. When he confiscated Arabic books in Granada, he had the medical books (about "thirty or forty volumes," according to Vallejo, *Memorial*, 35) set aside and sent to Alcalá; on another occasion he was given a number of idols abandoned by American Indians converted to the Christian faith: "horrible shapes of evil spirits, with eyes and teeth made of fishbone and ... legs and ears of cotton" (ibid., 45). At another time he sent to Alcalá a staff of exotic wood belonging to a Muslim kadi, seized in North Africa (ibid., 84). We also know from correspondence directed to him by university officials that Cisneros was consulted on the question of granting special leave to professors, and asked to read recommendations concerning new appointments and consider requests for remuneration above the regular salary. He was also kept informed about the quality of teaching and the number of students enrolled in certain courses. One letter written in 1512 supplies figures for students attending theology courses that year. There were slightly more Scotists (15) than Thomists (13). Overall attendance figures show that the university was still primarily an undergraduate institution, with more than two hundred enrolled in the basic *Summulae* course (de la Torre, "Universidad de Alcalá," 414–17).

Significantly, the history of scholarly publications at Alcalá is intricately linked with Cisneros' initiative. Earlier publications issuing from the local printer Stanislas Polono were exclusively in the vernacular. In 1510 Cisneros invited Arnao Guillén de Brocar of Logroño to establish a branch office in Alcalá. Although religious tracts, in Spanish and Latin, were its staple, the firm also issued numerous works of classical Greek and Roman authors, most of them critical editions by professors of the University of Alcalá. Among those produced between 1514 and 1530 were: Persius, Cicero, Plautus, Seneca, Curtius Rufus, Demosthenes, Isocrates, Xenophon, Libanius, Lucian, Cornelius Nepos, Valerius Flaccus, Quintilian, Caesar, and Plutarch. However, the most important work published by the firm of Guillèn de Brocar was the Polyglot Bible.

The Complutensian Polyglot

A by-product of Cisneros' promotion of the three biblical languages was the preparation of a polyglot edition of the Bible. According to Vallejo, the Cardinal first conceived of this ambitious project in 1502. It fit in well with his programme of religious reform, which included efforts to redirect and focus theology on the sources of Christian faith. Known by the Latin name for Alcalá as the "Complutensian Polyglot", the edition continued in the tradition of Origen's famous *Hexapla*, a multilingual version of the Old Testament. The Complutensian edition supplied, in parallel columns, the text of the complete Bible. It consisted of six folio volumes. The first four contained the Old Testament in Hebrew, Greek, and Latin, as well as the Chaldaic (Syriac) text for the Pentateuch. The fifth volume, which was printed first and bears a colophon of 10 January 1514, contained the Greek and Latin texts of the New Testament. Small reference letters denoted corresponding phrases in the Old Testament Hebrew and the Latin translation. The same practice was observed in the fifth volume, marking corresponding phrases in the New Testament Greek and the Latin translation. The ordinary Hebrew diacritics were omitted in print, as were the usual Greek accents and breathing marks. The sixth volume provided Hebrew and Chaldaic lexica and other study aids, such as a Hebrew grammar and interpretations of proper names. The printing was completed in 1517 (Volume Four bears the latest colophon date, 10 July 1517), but the editors delayed publication while awaiting papal authorization. This was obtained in March 1520. Shortly thereafter distribution of the books finally began.

Although Cisneros may have planned the project as early as Vallejo indicates, work does not seem to have begun in earnest until after Arnao Guillén de Brócar established his printing press in Alcalá. Guillén de Brócar, who had first set up shop in Pamplona and begun printing in 1490, had moved his press to Logroño in 1502. There he printed a number of works by Antonio Nebrija. The well-known philologist, who was also one of the collaborators on the Polyglot, may well have recommended Guillén de Brócar to the Cardinal. Although the printer already possessed a Greek type, it appears that he acquired in preparation for the new project (and perhaps with the financial aid of the Cardinal) two new Greek founts, as well as a new Roman and two Hebrew founts.

In the meantime Cisneros had assembled a group of distinguished scholars and was actively engaged in collecting and purchasing manuscript texts. According to his biographer, Gómez, he spent 4000 ducats on seven Hebrew manuscripts. The Prologue of the Polyglot states that the Greek and Latin manuscripts used were "neither of the common type or brought together without thought, but were the oldest and most correct exemplars, which our most holy lord, Pope Leo X, who favoured our enterprise, sent to us from the papal library. They were of such integrity that if one cannot fully trust them, there are seemingly no others worth consulting. We also used in addition a considerable number of other manuscripts, some of them copied with the greatest care from Bessarion's most correct codex and sent to us by the illustrious senate of Venice, others acquired by ourselves with great effort and at great expense from diverse places, so that we might have correct codices in abundance." For the Latin text the editors used manuscripts "of venerable age, but mostly those that are in the public library of our university at Alcalá, written more than eight hundred years ago in Gothic letters" (*Historical Catalogue*, 3). Unfortunately, only a few of the manuscripts used by the editors have been identified (Bentley, *Humanists*, 92–3).

The distribution of labour among the editors of the Polyglot remains a matter of some discussion (Bentley, *Humanists*, 74–91). It appears that the Hebrew text was the responsibility of the *conversos* Pablo Coronel and Alfonso de Zamora. The preparation of the Greek text was most likely entrusted to Hernán Núñez de Guzmán and Demetrios Ducas, the latter a native Cretan who had worked as an editor for the famous Aldine Press in Venice and more recently for Guillén de Brócar. Ducas was the only non-Spaniard on the editorial team. It was no doubt his experience and the quality of his work that recommended him to Cisneros. Other collaborators mentioned in the sources are Juan de Vergara and Diego López de Zúñiga, who may have worked on the preparation of the Vulgate. Vergara obtained his doctorate in theology at the university of Alcalá in 1517. As previously mentioned, he was Cisneros' secretary during the last two years of his life and was given canonries at Alcalá and Toledo. After Cisneros' death he remained in the service of his successor, Guillaume de Croÿ. López de Zúñiga, a graduate of Salamanca and a competent scholar in the biblical languages, became embroiled in controversies with the biblical humanists Jacques Lefèvre and Desiderius Erasmus, in whose translations and annotations he discovered "heresies". He pursued these polemics contrary to Cisneros' advice. After the Cardinal's death he moved to Rome and published his criticism in spite of prohibitions by the College of

Cardinals, making use of the confusion reigning after the death of Pope Adrian VI in 1523.

Best known among the editors was the philologist Elio Antonio de Nebrija, who moved to the University of Alcalá in 1513 from Salamanca, where he had occupied the chair of grammar. Nebrija (c. 1444–1522) had been exposed to humanism during his studies in Italy in the 1460s and brought a breath of the New Learning to Salamanca on his return. He emphasized that he had gone to Italy, not to further his career, but to further learning, "not to obtain a benefice or learn the formulae of civil and canon law, or do business, but … to restore the long lost authors of Latin, who have now been exiled from Spain for many centuries." Nebrija championed not only a revival of classical Latin, but also the purification of the vernacular. He did important studies on Spanish grammar, publishing a Latin-Spanish dictionary in 1492, and was accepted as an authority on philological questions. When he applied his knowledge to biblical studies, however, he aroused the suspicions of the Inquisitor-General, Diego de Deza, who confiscated his papers. Fortunately for Nebrija, Cisneros, who admired his scholarship, succeeded Deza in 1507. He released the papers to the author, who published them under the title of *Tertia Quinquagena*, that is, fifty annotations concerning biblical usage and the etymology of biblical names.

In an *Apologia* addressed to Cisneros, Nebrija defends himself against the accusation that he had dared to touch on theological matters, although he had no formal training in theology. He found it ironic that he could have chosen to write about literary trifles and enjoyed popularity, whereas choosing to write about serious matters close to every Christian's heart he had exposed himself to obloquy, was depicted as "a bold and sacrilegious falsifier" and came close to "being charged with impiety, shackled, and forced to defend [himself] in court." Nebrija insisted on the value of philology in establishing the correct text of the Bible: "Whenever there are variants in the Latin text of the New Testament, we must have recourse to the Greek manuscripts; whenever there is a disagreement among diverse Latin manuscripts or between the Latin and Greek manuscripts of the Old Testament, we must apply the standard of the Hebrew original" (Nebrija, *Apologia*, a1 verso–a2 verso).

In 1513 Cisneros invited Nebrija to join the team of biblical scholars working on the Polyglot edition of the Bible. He did not remain a member of the team for very long, however, since he could not agree with fellow editors on matters of editorial policy. In a letter tendering his resignation Nebrija explained that he disagreed with the decision to include Remigius' etymological lexicon of names, which he did not consider philologically adequate. More importantly, he rejected the practice followed by the team of establishing the Latin text by collating Latin manuscripts only rather than correcting them against the original Greek. It had been his understanding, Nebrija wrote, that he "was to take part in the correction of the Latin which is commonly corrupted in all the Latin Bibles, by comparing it with the Hebrew, Chaldaic, and Greek" (*Revista de Archivos, Bibliotecas y Museos* 8 [1903], 495). Nebrija's remarks imply that the team followed (and the Cardinal endorsed) a policy of keeping the language traditions separate, that is, of collating only same-language manuscripts. The published text of the Complutensian Bible does not entirely support Nebrija's complaint, as we shall see.

Cisneros also attempted to attract Desiderius Erasmus, the most renowned biblical humanist north of the Alps. In November 1516 the abbot of Husillos wrote to Cisneros, praising Erasmus' edition of the New Testament, which had just appeared from the Froben press. The author, he said, was a good theologian, knowledgeable in Greek and Hebrew (in the latter he was mistaken), and an elegant Latin stylist. He suggested that his experience might benefit the editors of the Complutensian Polyglot: "Given that he has anticipated Your Reverence with his publication, I believe that he could be of assistance in making your work appear somewhat more polished ... I believe that Your Reverence should not deprive yourself of a person like Erasmus. You should avail yourself of his assistance in the correction of the whole publication and hire his services for a certain period" (Bataillon, *Erasmo*, 72, n. 1).

Erasmus mentions an invitation from the Cardinal, but says that he declined it (*Epistolae*, ed. Allen, 582:9). Cisneros appears to have persisted, and in May 1517 Erasmus laconically states the reason for a second refusal: "The Cardinal of Toledo has invited me again, but I do not like Spain" (Ep. 598:47-8). In 1527 Juan Vergara refers to the matter in a letter to Erasmus, recalling that "Cardinal Cisneros, the founder of the Complutensian university, ... had the most wonderful esteem for you and was keen on enjoying your company" (Ep. 1814:459-61). Perhaps Erasmus was wise not to accept the invitation.

It is likely that his relationship with colleagues on the project would not have been smooth. We have already mentioned López de Zúñiga's criticism of Erasmus' work, which resulted in a prolonged polemic between the two scholars. Nebrija, too, found fault with the annotations in Erasmus' New Testament edition. Of this, however, Erasmus did not become aware until after Nebrija's death, when the imperial secretary Guy Morillon sent him a critical note in Nebrija's hand. Erasmus was clearly annoyed. "I would have thought Nebrija was more open-minded ... it is a quarrel over goat's wool," was his miffed reply (Gilly, *El Erasmismo en España*, 195–218).

Cisneros saw the completion of the work under his direction, but not its publication. Modern scholars speculate that the editors delayed publication because Pope Leo had granted Erasmus' publisher, Johann Froben, an exclusive privilege for four years. Waiting for the papal imprimatur, however, had more than legal significance. It provided the work with much-needed protection against critics of the enterprise. The application of philology to biblical studies was suffering from the stigma of heterodoxy. Several factors had contributed to this perception. First of all, textual criticism of the Bible, which in turn led to reinterpretations of some passages, was seen as part of a reform movement which under Luther's leadership was developing into a schismatic movement. Secondly, edition and translation was claimed by humanists as their task proper, whereas theologians insisted on the exclusive right to deal with biblical texts. The interference of "theologizing humanists", especially their efforts to translate the Bible into vernacular languages, was considered a violation of the teaching authority of the church. Thirdly, traditionalists saw any revision of the biblical text as tampering with the Word of God and a challenge to the principle of inspiration. Yet, as the medieval trivium gave way to more comprehensive humanistic studies and philology became a focal point of the curriculum, scholars became increasingly aware of the fact that the Bible, like other texts, had been corrupted over time through the negligence of scribes. In Italy Lorenzo Valla and in northern Europe Erasmus and Lefèvre attempted to rescue the original text, but their textual criticism met with stiff resistance from more traditional elements in the church. Their work was seen as an inspirational source of the reformers and thus, in the eyes of adherents to the old faith, was connected with heterodoxy.

In the preface to the Polyglot, addressed to Pope Leo X, Cisneros therefore justified his enterprise and explained his motives for producing the edition:

> There are many reasons, Holy Father, that impel us to print the text of Holy Scripture in the original languages. These are the principal ones. Words have their own unique character, and no translation of them, however complete, can entirely express their full meaning ... they are laden with a variety of sublime truths which cannot be understood from any source other than the original language. Moreover, wherever there is diversity in the Latin manuscripts or the suspicion of a corrupted reading (we know how frequently this occurs because of the ignorance and negligence of copyists), it is necessary to go back to the original source of Scripture, as St. Jerome and St. Augustine and other ecclesiastical writers advise us to do, to examine the authenticity of the books of the Old Testament in light of the original Hebrew text and of the New Testament in light of the Greek copies. And so that every student of Holy Scripture might have at hand the original texts themselves and be able to quench his thirst at the very fountainhead of the water that flows unto life everlasting and not have to content himself with rivulets alone, we ordered the original languages of Holy Scripture with their translations adjoined to be printed. (Olin, *Catholic Reformation*, 62–3)

Cisneros' dedicatory letter contains a remarkable number of parallels with Erasmus' prolegomena to his New Testament edition. Erasmus likewise deplored the negligence of scribes and emphasized the care and effort involved in obtaining and collating "old and very correct" manuscripts. He, too, cited Augustine and Jerome for the need to consult the original texts, "the actual sources, rather than pools and runnels" to discover the hidden meaning of the divine words (*CWE*, Epp. 384, 373). Chronological considerations would suggest that Cisneros was inspired by Erasmus' words, but there is no need to postulate a dependence since both men faced the same potential criticism and were bound to offer similar justifications. Their arguments can, moreover, be traced to the letters and prefaces of Jerome, who had to defend his philological work against much the same criticism (Rummel, *Humanist-Scholastic Debate*, 100–102).

Nebrija's letter of resignation implied that Cisneros' team kept the language traditions separate. The Cardinal's preface says nothing about his editorial principles but clearly states that he expected readers to compare the translation with the original. An inspection of the text shows, moreover, that it was not consistently based on a collation of same-language manuscripts. Jerry Bentley, who examined the Polyglot text of the New Testament in some detail, noted that the Latin Vulgate was occasionally emended on the basis of the Greek text. More typically, however, the editors chose among the Greek variants those that agreed with the Latin Vulgate. In one notorious case, they supplied the Greek for 1 John 5:7 (the "Comma Johanneum"), for which they could find no manuscript evidence, by retranslating the Latin Vulgate. Bentley concluded that "anarchy reigned over principle in the editing of the Polyglot edition" (Bentley, *Humanists*, 107). It should be added, however, that anarchy reigned in many editions at a time when textual criticism was in its infancy.

The practice of inserting a passage for which there was no manuscript evidence, for example, strikes the modern scholar as inexcusable. Yet Erasmus, the most admired textual critic of his time, resorted to the same practice and nonchalantly observed: "Since I found at the end of this book [of Revelation] a few words in our Vulgate which were missing in the Greek manuscripts, I added them out of the Latin" (*Novum Instrumentum* [1516], II, 625). His candid admission implies that he saw nothing wrong with this practice. Bentley observes that the Polyglot edition did not manifest "careful, professional editorial scholarship" (Bentley, *Humanists*, 110); Erasmus has likewise been accused of shoddy editorial practices. Nevertheless modern scholars agree that the two editions are hallmarks in the history of biblical scholarship and recognize that the editors cannot be held to the standards of modern textual criticism. They were hampered by limited access to manuscripts, by the novelty of the task, which they learned by doing, and by a culture that regarded any challenge to tradition as inherently evil. No doubt, biblical humanists had to overcome scruples, in themselves and in their readers, when their findings contradicted traditional exegesis.

It is for this reason that Cisneros' editors did not consistently emend the Vulgate and Erasmus refrained from radical changes to the Latin text in his first edition of the New Testament, commenting: "I did it sparingly, fearing that some people would not tolerate such innovation" (*Novum Testamentum* [1519], B4 recto). Erasmus sought to protect his reputation by adding copious annotations explaining his editorial decisions. They did not produce the intended effect, however. On the contrary, far from justifying the editor in the eyes of the readers, the annotations involved Erasmus in a series of polemics. His work was investigated by the Spanish Inquisition and formally condemned by the Faculty of Theology at Paris. The editors of the Polyglot, by contrast, supplied only brief marginal notes, providing mostly biblical cross-references and defining unusual words. Only a handful of marginal notes addressed textual problems. In light of Erasmus' experience, the restraint of the Polyglot editors appears prudent.

From a commercial point of view the Polyglot was not a success, but then Cisneros had not looked for material profit, as the executors of his estate explained. The price was set, "not counting the expenses, which were practically endless, but the benefit derived from reading the text" (*Historical Catalogue*, 3). According to estimates Cisneros had expended some 50,000 gold ducats on printing and research costs. Of the six hundred sets printed, a considerable number was lost in a shipwreck; the remainder were sold for six and a half ducats each. About 150 sets survive today. The rise of humanism had generated a lively interest in polyglot editions, but the Basel printer Johann Froben had anticipated the Complutensian Polyglot with the bilingual edition of the New Testament prepared and annotated by Erasmus. Published in 1516, the Erasmian text had gained a strong foothold in the market place long before the Polyglot reached the stage of publication. The Erasmian New Testament retained its hold on the readership. Unlike the comprehensive Complutensian Polyglot, it went through five editions between 1516 and 1535, and proved an eminently "saleable commodity" (*CWE*, Ep. 1010).

5 Cisneros and the Politics of Spain, 1492–1516

Cisneros' political influence developed with his appointment as the Queen's confessor and his elevation shortly thereafter to the archbishopric of Toledo, a position that entailed the primacy of Spain. He was present and no doubt played a role in the negotiations preceding the marriage alliances between the Spanish Crown and the Habsburgs which provided for the double union of Margaret and Philip the Handsome, the children of Emperor Maximilian, with Juan and Juana, the children of the Catholic Monarchs.

The homeland of the Habsburgs was the Upper Rhine region and Austria, but the focus of Habsburg politics changed in 1477, when Maximilian secured the hand of Mary, the heiress of Burgundy. As regent of Burgundy on his wife's behalf, Maximilian held fiefs from both the French Crown and the German Empire. On the accidental death of his wife, their son Philip the Handsome inherited the title to Burgundy. He was declared of age in 1494 and invested as Duke. Shortly afterwards the marriage contracts linking the Habsburgs with the Spanish crown were signed.

In 1496 Cisneros accompanied the Queen to Burgos to make arrangements for the departure of Princess Juana for Burgundy, where her marriage to Philip was celebrated on 21 October. In 1497 he performed the marriage ceremony uniting the crown prince Juan with Margaret of Austria. The same year saw the marriage of another of the royal princesses, Isabel, to Manuel I of Portugal. Negotiations also continued for the marriage of Princess Catherine to Arthur, crown prince of England, and after his death, to his brother Henry (later Henry VIII).

When Juan, the only son and designated heir of the Monarchs, died unexpectedly in October 1497 at the age of nineteen, the scale of the funeral was proportionate to the sense of loss experienced by his parents. The Burgundian historian Philippe de Commines, who devoted a chapter in his *Memoirs* (8.24) to the misfortunes of the Spanish royal family, commented that he had never heard of such intense manifestations of public grief. "For forty days all commerce came to a stop ... everyone wore coarse black cloth, and the nobility and men of stature had their mules decked out completely in black down to their knees — only the eyes were visible — and black banners covered the doors of houses in the cities." National grief was also given expression in the famous musical setting of "Triste España sin ventura" by Juan del Encina.

The carefully laid plans for the Spanish succession were further disturbed, when Margaret's pregnancy ended in a stillbirth later that year. The succession now devolved on Isabel, the oldest daughter of the Catholic Monarchs, but with her death the following year and that of her infant son in 1500, the right of succession passed to Juana and Philip the Handsome. The couple had been residing in Brussels and Ghent, where Juana had given birth to two daughters, Eleanor and Isabel, and to a son, Charles. Her husband's philandering and her own violently jealous reactions had marred the marital peace during these years, however.

The couple arrived in Spain in January 1502 to formalize their right of succession. On this occasion, too, Cisneros was in attendance, presiding over their installation in a solemn ceremony at the cathedral of Toledo and remaining with the royal family during the following five months, "without however paying much attention to the court festivities", as Gómez duly notes (Retana, *Cisneros*, 114). The pageant with which the couple was received is described in detail in a panegyric addressed to the Duke by one of his Burgundian subjects, the humanist Desiderius Erasmus: "In the cathedral of Toledo, which is dedicated to the Virgin, before a congregation formed of the flower of the Spanish nobility, witnessed by every high dignitary of the ecclesiastical order, by the grace of God, in the presence of the king and queen surrounded by a vast crowd of civil officials and magistrates, you were installed and crowned with solemn ceremony as ruler of Castile; and allegiance was sworn to you with wonderful unanimity and an enthusiasm never known before ... Thus you filled Spain to overflowing with an accumulation of joy" (*CWE* 27, pp. 24–5).

This was the official version; in reality Philip and his Flemish advisors were highly unpopular. He spoke no Spanish and had no understanding of Spanish tradition, giving offense to many with his cavalier behaviour. It was, moreover, interpreted as a lack of commitment that he could not be persuaded to remain in Spain, either to accommodate his pregnant wife whose condition did not allow her to return to Flanders, or to become better acquainted with the customs of the people he was to rule. There was also unease about Philip's relations with France. King Louis XII had given him a magnificent reception on his journey through France, which included a ceremonial session with the Paris Parlement, a gesture welcomed by the francophile Flemish party accompanying the Duke. Such demonstrations of friendship flew in the face of Spanish sentiments. In a candid letter to his ambassador in London Ferdinand gave vent to his anger about Philip's attitude. "I spoke at length with [Philip], advising him not to leave the country. There were many reasons: first, in case of my wife's, the Queen's, death, my daughter, the princess, and he must immediately take peaceful possession of these realms; secondly ... in spite of the advice and counter to the wishes expressed by myself and my wife the Queen he departed, travelling right through the territory of the French King — his and my enemy — putting himself into his hands." Subsequently Philip joined in an alliance with France, which was clearly not in the interest of Spain: "He made the French allies his allies and the French enemies his enemies, without including or excepting us and our realm, thus putting at risk my rights in Naples and favouring those of the French king in this treaty of friendship" (Díaz-Plaja, *Historia de España*, 50). Similarly the English ambassadors in Spain reported in 1506 that "the people were sorry that [Philip] was so much ruled by the Council of France" (Bergenroth, *Letters and Papers*, I #437).

It was on less than cordial terms, then, that Philip departed for Flanders at the end of February 1503. His wife Juana remained in Toledo, where she gave birth one month later to a son, Ferdinand. Cisneros baptized the child and, taking advantage of the fact that the prince was born in his diocese, obtained from the Queen a tax exemption for Toledo (Gómez, *De rebus gestis*, 135).

The Death of Queen Isabel (1504)

In the following year Queen Isabel died at the age of fifty-three. Although Cisneros was not present at her death in November 1504, he was one of the executors of the will, which made Juana Queen of

Castile and Leon. Cisneros' biographer, Gómez de Castro, notes that Juana's husband was all but excluded from power, "whether the Queen [Isabel] harboured hostile feelings on account of his unworthy treatment of her daughter or because she really thought that he was ill prepared to govern Spain" (Gómez, *De rebus gestis*, 153). In her will Isabel merely noted that obedience was owed to Philip by Juana's subjects "as her husband" (Díaz-Plaja, *Historia de España*, 40). However, she also acknowledged the need for contingency plans, taking into consideration Juana's mental imbalance. In case she proved incapable of exercising government, the will provided that Ferdinand was to assume the regency until his oldest grandson (Charles, then four years old) had reached the age of twenty. The Queen carefully noted that she had taken the advice of the *cortes* as well as of "some prelates and grandees of my kingdom" and that "all had been in agreement" on this point (ibid.). The provisions of Isabel's will were promulgated at the *cortes* of Toro in March 1505 and confirmed at Salamanca in November of that year. Philip, however, did not accept the passive role envisaged for him, and the interpretation of the will became the subject of prolonged and tenacious negotiations with his father-in-law.

Philip's bid for power was supported by Castilian nobles who were willing to intrigue on his behalf against the "old Catalan", as the unpopular Ferdinand was dubbed. In the words of Pietro Martire "the nobles grunt and sharpen their teeth like wild boars with the desire and hope of a great change" (Ep. 277). Similarly, the English ambassadors in Spain reported to their king, Henry VII, that factions existed and "there is fear of troubles ensuing". At the same time they noted that Ferdinand's position in Aragon was secure and that he was *de facto* in control of Castile: "All the nobles and commons [in Aragon] are very obedient, loving him for the good justice he ministers to them ... Immediately on his Queen's decease he had proclaimed himself Governor and Administrator of Castile on behalf of his daughter, ... and received all the revenues for his own use" (Bergenroth, *Letters and Papers*, I #437, July 1505). Ferdinand had, moreover, scored a diplomatic victory by concluding peace with France (Blois, October 1505) and marrying Germaine de Foix, niece of the French King Louis XII (cf. Díaz-Plaja, *Historia de España*, 50-1). The marriage contract provided that the crown of Aragon would pass to the heirs of Germaine and Ferdinand, and that parts of

Naples should be handed over to Germaine and were to revert to France if she died childless. Ferdinand explained the diplomatic import of his actions: "The Archduke, my son, ... has made demonstrations of desiring to come to Spain with an army and a fleet. I, therefore, seeing that he had made a league with the King of France so greatly to my prejudice, and in order that no inconvenience might ensue to me from the said league, also that I might the better provide for the preservation of these kingdoms, and of my honour and my rights, have agreed to a treaty of peace and amity and brotherhood with the King of France for the preservation of our realms ... I have now sent to beg and request [Philip] to study and determine who is entitled to rule these kingdoms, in order that peace may not be disturbed. For though the government of them belongs to me, and they have sworn fealty and obedience to me, and are at peace, yet he pretends that the said government belongs to him" (Bergenroth, *Letters and Papers*, I #450, December 1505).

A compromise was eventually reached and a treaty signed at Salamanca (26 December 1505), which provided for a tripartite government of Castile, dividing authority between Juana, Philip, and Ferdinand. Documents were to be signed "Don Fernando, Don Felipe, Doña Juana, by the grace of God Kings and princes of Castile, Leon, Aragon, the two Sicilies, Jerusalem, Granada, etc., Archdukes of Austria, Dukes of Burgundy". The signatories were to be referred to as "Their Highnesses," a title until then reserved for Queen Juana (Díaz-Plaja, *Historia de España*, 52–3).

A second round of negotiations took place in the spring of 1506, however, after Philip's arrival in Spain with an army of three thousand Flemish and German soldiers. During these negotiations, Cisneros acted as Ferdinand's liaison. He had advised Ferdinand to rely on military force in turn (García Oro, *Cisneros*, 150), but the King's weak position in Castile obliged him to negotiate. On 2 June Ferdinand sent Cisneros to a meeting with Philip, giving the Archbishop plenary powers to act on his behalf and, as the document stated, "to sign in my name and in my absence any agreement with the Most Serene King Philip, my very dear and dearly beloved son, in all matters necessary for the true and perpetual union and concord between him and myself." He declared his desire to remove any reason for distrust, "for they say, among other things, that the said Most Serene King, my son, fears that I shall conspire against him with the Most

Serene Queen, my daughter, his wife". He protested that he had "no desire to act against him or to his prejudice, but rather to collaborate with them [Philip and Juana] in love and peace and agreement" (Díaz-Plaja, *Historia de España*, 55–6). There was, however, little room for maneuvering since Philip enjoyed the support of a great part of the Castilian nobility. Ferdinand was therefore obliged on 28 June 1506 to sign the agreement of Villafáfila, handing over the government of Castile to his "beloved children" and promising to retire to Aragon. In the agreement he emphasized that he was relinquishing his power voluntarily to avoid war and dissension, because he "wished to put peace and the common weal of the kingdom before his private interest" (ibid., 57). The document also contained a mutual defense pact between Philip and Ferdinand. According to Cisneros' biographer Gómez de Castro, the archbishop was apologetic about his inability to bring about a settlement more favourable to Ferdinand. In a letter to the regent, he said "that although the agreement was not to be despised, it did not satisfy him, but since he could not obtain more, he accepted the conditions which weren't all that bad" (Gómez, *De rebus gestis*, 170). Ferdinand himself protested that the treaty was prejudicial to him, but acknowledged that he was forced to accept the conditions because Philip had "assembled the grandees [of Castile] and united a powerful and strong army, so that my royal person is in notorious and manifest danger ... thus from fear and apprehension of what has been stated and, ... since the said King, my son-in-law, is determined entirely to usurp, as in fact he does, the administration of these kingdoms, despoiling me of the administration which on many accounts belongs to me by right ... I am obliged to sign" (Bergenroth, *Letters and Papers*, II, 1509–1525, #12, 27 June 1506).

Letters to his ambassadors in England and Venice project the image Ferdinand wanted to present to the world: the unselfish and loving father, who was doing everything to foster peace and whose intentions were misinterpreted or misrepresented by a grasping son-in-law. To the English court he wrote: "Having found that the peace and tranquillity of these kingdoms could not otherwise be sufficiently provided for, I have entered into a treaty with the Archduke [Philip]. For I always desire the welfare of my children on account of the love I bear them" (Bergenroth, *Letters and Papers*, I, #471, summer 1506). To his ambassador in Venice he wrote in a similar vein.

He had always cherished fatherly feelings toward Philip, but "enemies whispered into Juana's ears that he intended to retain for himself the royal prerogatives of the crown of Castile." He noted that he
was in fact "entitled to do so by the will of the late Queen, but
never had the desire to make use of that right during the lifetime of
Philip and Juana." He complained, moreover, that Philip had acted
like an enemy. On his arrival in Spain, "instead of hastening to see
their father, they sent messengers to him and asked him to appoint
a formal meeting ... Philip even thought it proper to come to the
meeting with an armed guard" (Bergenroth, *Letters and Papers*, I,
#470, 1 July 1506). English documents meanwhile tell a different
story, showing Ferdinand intriguing against Philip and encouraging
French support for the rebellious Duke of Guelders in the hope that
his operations in Burgundy would oblige Philip to leave Spain and
return home (ibid., #477, July 1506).

In the event, Ferdinand did not retire to Aragon, as he had
announced, but instead departed for Naples, to secure his position
there. The kingdom had been conquered in 1443 by Ferdinand's
uncle, Alfonso I, who became joint ruler of Naples and Sicily. After
his death in 1458, Sicily passed into the hands of Ferdinand's father
and subsequently to himself. Naples, which was claimed by France,
was retained, after a long struggle, by Ferrante, Alfonso's illegitimate
son and Ferdinand's brother-in-law. He repeatedly received military
aid from Ferdinand, who maintained the alliance in his own interest,
for the protection of Sicily. After Ferrante's death, the French king
Charles VIII revived claims to the kingdom. He invaded Italy in 1494
and briefly occupied Naples, which was, however, recovered by Ferrantino, Ferrante's grandson, with the help of the Spanish Gran Capitán
Gonzálo de Córdoba. Ferrantino enjoyed his victory only briefly, dy-
ing unexpectedly in 1496 and leaving the kingdom in the hands of his
uncle Frederick. In these circumstances both France and Spain pressed
their respective claims and found it convenient to unite their forces.
They jointly invaded Naples and partitioned it in 1501. Very soon,
however, a dispute arose between Ferdinand and Charles' successor,
Louis XII. Spanish troops drove out the French and made Ferdinand
the sole ruler of Naples in 1504. Subsequently it was governed by
viceroys appointed by the Spanish Crown. The terms of Ferdinand's
marriage contract with Germaine de Foix, which allowed for a hypo-
thetical reversal of Naples to France, represented a rapprochement.

On arrival in Naples in 1506, Ferdinand's first act was to relieve the viceroy, Gonzalo de Córdoba, whose loyalty he suspected, and take over the reins of government himself. Fortune then took a rapid turn in his favour: Philip fell ill and died in September 1506, leaving a power vacuum.

Cisneros' First Regency (1506/7)

Already during the last days of Philip's illness, Cisneros' house became a meeting place for power brokers. After Philip's death a hastily formed interim council, presided over by Cisneros, proposed recalling Ferdinand but also expressed fear of his resentment. According to Gómez, Pimentel, Señor de Benavente, voiced his concern: "Are you not aware that, remembering the recent confrontation, he will treat all of us with insolence? And being a master of dissimulating his innermost feelings, he will be full of benevolence on the outside and smile sweetly at first and will punish us severely later?" (Gómez, *De rebus gestis*, 185) The chronicler Pero Mexía reports that among the alternatives discussed was the suggestion that "the kingdom be governed by the council in the name of Juana" (Mexía, *Cronica*, 41). Others advanced the idea that the Emperor Maximilian be approached and made regent on behalf of his grandson Charles. Cisneros, however, spoke against calling in a stranger and reminded them that Ferdinand was an experienced and competent ruler.

The hectic nature of the negotiations in the days following Philip's death is illustrated by an anecdote related by Cisneros' biographer, Juan Vallejo. After an interminable meeting, the archbishop ordered dinner to be served, but was reminded by his valet that it was now past midnight and by eating at this time he would be in technical violation of the church law requiring abstinence from food before morning mass. According to Vallejo, the archbishop demonstrated his quick mind and diplomatic skills by insisting: "Have dinner served. It cannot possibly be more than eleven o'clock." No one contradicted the archbishop.

Cisneros' proposal to recall Ferdinand was accepted by the council in the end. He was formally appointed guardian of the Queen and representative of crown prince Charles' interests until Ferdinand's return. The Queen had formally been asked her opinion, but after Philip's death she had abandoned herself to grief and was unwilling or unable to make political decisions. The disconcerting behaviour of the widow is reported in some detail by Pietro Martire. The Queen, seeking solace in a convent at Tordesillas, wished to take her husband's corpse with her.

> The Archbishop of Burgos met with her and explained to the Queen that this was forbidden ... She had a fit of anger and obstinately persisted in her wish. She ordered her servants to open the grave and take out the coffin. None of the nobles or prelates could make her desist from her purpose. All were of the opinion that one must not put pressure on her for fear that another fit of anger might cause her to abort the fetus she was carrying in her uterus. Thus they disinterred the corpse of her husband on December 20. We saw it placed into a container of lead, covered with another of wood, in the presence of all the ambassadors. ... We made the journey with the corpse being transported in a carriage and four, escorting the coffin, covered with a royal cloth of silk and gold. We stopped in Torquemada ... armed soldiers guarded the corpse in the parish church, as if enemies were on the point of assaulting the walls. Women were strictly forbidden to enter. She was plagued by the same jealousy as during her husband's lifetime.

The following day the company proceeded toward the village of Hornillos. On the way they encountered a convent.

> Thinking that it was the house of friars, the Queen ordered suddenly to halt the cortege and lower the coffin to the ground in open country. But when she realized that it was a women's convent, she immediately gave orders to transport the coffin elsewhere. On the open road, at night, she commanded that the bearers take the corpse out of the coffin by the uncertain light of torches, which could barely be kept ablaze because of a strong wind. Some carpenters, fetched for this purpose, opened the wooden and lead containers. After contemplating the corpse of her husband and calling on the nobles as witnesses, she ordered them to close it anew and transport it to Hornillos on their shoulders. (quoted Díaz Plaja, *Historia de España*, 60)

The monastery at Tordesillas became the final resting place for the corpse, and Juana remained there in a state of deep melancholy until her own death in 1555.

The bizarre behaviour of the disturbed Queen on this and other occasions soon made clear that Ferdinand's plans for her future, which included remarriage, were unrealistic. As soon as she was widowed, the English king, Henry VII, showed interest in a dynastic union. According to a letter from Ferdinand to his councillor and secretary, Miguel Perez Almazan, the English did not mind her derangement "as long as it did not prevent her from bearing children" (Bergenroth, *Letters and Papers*, Vol. 1, #511, April 1507). Ferdinand warned Henry, however, that the subject must be broached to her by none but himself. Only he knew how to handle her. At one point Henry suggested to use the services of Cisneros and asked his daugher-in-law, Catherine, to write a letter to this effect. She had a direct interest in the affair, since her marriage to the English crown prince was held up by Ferdinand's reluctance to pay the remainder of her dowry. If the marriage between Juana and the king could be brought about, he was willing to make concessions regarding her dowry. Catherine, however, was uncertain about taking the initiative in such a delicate matter and asked her father for further directions (ibid., #541, 7 Sept 1507). Henry also held out hopes of financing an expedition against Africa jointly with Ferdinand and the King of Portugal, once the marriage to Juana was concluded (ibid., #552, October 1507). On his return to Spain, Ferdinand did in fact broach the subject to Juana. He reported to his ambassador at the English court that her mental state was still precarious, that she assured him of her filial devotion but asked him not to force her into a new marriage. He desisted from importuning her further because he was convinced his efforts would be in vain. It is unclear to what extent, if any, Cisneros was personally involved in attempts to obtain the Queen's agreement. Shortly afterwards the English king refocused his marriage plans on Juan's widow, Margaret, with a similar lack of success.

To return to the year 1506: the unpredictability of the Queen and her unwillingness to involve herself in matters of government created considerable difficulties for Cisneros. His executive power rested on uncertain legal grounds, and insurrection was a distinct danger. An accord signed on October 1 by the archbishop and council members reflects their fear of civil war. They agreed to refrain from the following actions: interference with the established norms of administration; the recruiting of military forces; efforts to gain power over the persons of Juana or her son Ferdinand. They furthermore agreed to abide by majority decisions made by the council. Cisneros had been delegated to write to Ferdinand asking him to return and once more take over the regency of the country until Charles, the heir to the throne, would come of age. According to Vallejo, he asked Ferdinand "not to think of the past and of the passions of the nobility, but putting all aside, to come as quickly as possible and take over the government like a true Lord and Father ... for there was no other, besides God, to remedy this great loss and misfortune" (resume of letter in Gómez, *De rebus gestis*, 188–9). It appears that Cisneros had hoped to obtain plenipotentiary powers from Juana for himself. A document to this effect was drawn up (García Oro, *Cisneros*, 160, n. 16), but remained unsigned.

While Ferdinand attended to his affairs in Naples, Spain sank into civil war and was convulsed by rebellion. The Duke of Medina Sidonia attempted to regain Gibraltar, which had been taken from him by the Crown in 1502; the Count of Lemos, similarly deprived, briefly retook Ponferrada in Galicia; feuds broke out in Segovia, Toledo, and Madrid. In Granada the soldiers mutinied, and in Córdoba the prisoners of the Inquisition were released. An outbreak of the plague added to the chaos. Pietro Martire predicted that "everything will collapse" (Ep. 354).

After Ferdinand's return to Spain in August 1507, order was restored, as he reported with great satisfaction to his daughter Catherine: "They told me ... that my arrival was necessary for the welfare and restoration of the Most Serene Queen my dearly beloved daughter and your dear sister, and for the good of this realm, which, before my arrival, was without order and in great upheaval and tumult" (Díaz-Plaja, *Historia de España*, 62). The *cortes* officially delegated authority to Ferdinand. He in turn brought with him from Italy papal briefs making Cisneros a cardinal and naming him Inquisitor General of Spain.

Spain under Ferdinand, 1507–1516

The following years saw the expedition to Oran, which has already been discussed in the context of Cisneros' missionary efforts. The Cardinal retained his position of authority at court and repeatedly acted as Ferdinand's representative during periods of absence: in 1510, when Ferdinand attended the *cortes* of Aragon, he left Cisneros in charge of his daughter and grandson Ferdinand; in 1511 and 1512 he called for his presence to discuss diplomatic negotiations and military preparations in connection with the Holy League concluded between Spain, England, the Empire, and the Pope against France. The year 1512 also saw the invasion and annexation of Navarre.

The Conquest of Navarre

Navarre, wedged between France and Aragon, had once been the possession of Ferdinand's father, John II of Aragon, through his marriage with Blanche, Queen of Navarre. On his death it passed through his daughter first to the family of Foix and, when that line had no male issue, to the family of Albret. However, in a series of treaties between 1476 and 1500 Navarre became effectively a Spanish protectorate and thus was destined to be annexed. The final steps in that direction were taken in July 1512, when Ferdinand used the rivalry between the Foix and Albret families to put in a claim on behalf of his wife, Germaine de Foix. Alleging that there existed a secret French plan to invade Aragon through Navarre, he ventured a pre-emptive strike in July 1512. He was aided by both the English king and the pope. Henry VII was persuaded to send an army to Guienne to recover ancient English possessions, thus preventing France from coming to the aid of Navarre. Pope Julius II, allied with Ferdinand in the Holy League, excommunicated the Navarrese King, Jean d'Albret, because he had supported the schismatic Council of Pisa. Within a few months Navarre was conquered by Spanish troops under the command of the Duke of Alba and annexed to Aragon. This arrangement was changed in 1515, when Navarre was incorporated in Castile, while retaining a certain amount of autonomy in its administration and coinage.

According to Gómez, Cisneros' presence at the deliberations leading up to the conquest lent legitimacy to the proceedings: "In August he once again was at the side of the king, who was in Logroño, occupied with the problems of Navarre. His interest in what is good and just was always so strong, his consideration for religion so great, that by the mere presence of such a man the war could seem just" (*De rebus gestis*, 354). Cisneros' exact role or involvement in Ferdinand's plans are, however, difficult to assess.

The military and diplomatic success in Navarre did not suffice to improve Ferdinand's relations with the Castilian nobility. They continued to intrigue against him. The malcontents found receptive ears

at the Burgundian court. Ferdinand's position in Castile was therefore still precarious when he died in January 1516. For some time he
had wrestled with the question of succession. Personally he inclined
toward his younger grandson and namesake Ferdinand, with whom
he had a closer relationship than with Charles who was brought up
in Burgundy. In the end, however, he made Charles the heir. Gómez
second-guessed his motives: "He was easily persuaded not to put
Ferdinand in charge of the kingdom because he was convinced that
Charles, educated in the Belgian tradition, would never come to
Spain" (*De rebus gestis*, 370).

6 The Second Regency, 1516–1517

The immediate problem confronting the advisors assembled at Ferdinand's deathbed was the appointment of a regent. Ferdinand's natural son, Alonso, Archbishop of Zaragoza, was to assume that function in Aragon. With regard to Castile, however, "the choice was difficult and critical," Gómez writes.

> It was not recommendable to name one of the nobles on account of their old established and deep rivalries, nor someone of modest situation and fortune, for it was a characteristic of the Spaniards not to accept as ruler anyone who was not a grandee. It was difficult, moreover, for a man accustomed to deal with small matters to speedily grow into his new role and be equal to such an important task. ... [When Cisneros' name was put forward], the King turned his head in a manner that indicated his misgivings and gave them to understand that the proposal did not please him. And his words confirmed his thoughts. "Do you not know Cisneros' character?" [he asked]. "He is not equal to dealing with men of such diverse conditions." But when he noticed that all remained silent at his question, he changed, it seems, as if by divine inspiration, and said: "If I could design for myself a man equal to the task, I would prefer Cisneros to be more manageable and reasonable. Customs have changed for the worse; to demand that men conform with the old rigorous standards of honour, which Cisneros himself upholds, will cause great problems in the realm. On the other hand I am inclined to accept your proposal because I know his integrity, his spirit, and his mind which is always desirous of that which is right and just; I also know that he is not related to any nobleman and will not be constrained by private causes and friendships. Moreover, the favours granted him by Isabel and myself have put him under an obligation and made him our

partisan. Or, to put it another way, he is much obliged to us, of which he has given clear proof in many instances." Those present applauded the king's words and thanked him for choosing Cisneros. (Gómez, *De rebus gestis*, 371–2)

Ferdinand's will accordingly named as his successor Charles, who was "to govern and administrate the realm on behalf of the Most Serene Queen, the Lady Juana, his mother and our most dear and beloved daughter." Cisneros was appointed regent of Castile in the absence of Charles, so "that the said Cardinal might do what we would do or have the authority or obligation to do, until Charles decides on a course of action, ... trusting in his conscience, religion, rectitude and good will" (will, quoted Retana, *Cisneros*, 2:20–1). Ferdinand died on 23 January 1516 in Madrigalejo near Guadalupe, at an inn where he had taken lodging. When the Royal Council communicated the provisions of the will to Charles' representative, Adrian of Utrecht, the clause "until Prince Charles decides on a course of action" was suppressed. The cardinal's regency was to remain in place until Charles could come to Spain in person.

Charles had grown up at the court of his aunt Margaret, Regent of the Netherlands. When his parents, Philip and Juana, departed for Spain in 1506, to claim Juana's inheritance, they left the six-year old Charles and his sisters Eleanor, Mary, and Isabel in the care of Philip's sister, Margaret. She conducted affairs from her castle in Mechelen near Brussels, where the royal offspring received a careful education and were groomed for their future tasks. Each of the children was destined to play a role in the politics of Europe: Charles was to inherit the realms of his grandparents and succeed Maximilian as emperor; Eleanor was to become Queen of Portugal and, through her second marriage, of France; Mary and Isabel were to become Queens of Hungary and Denmark respectively. The siblings were brought up in the Burgundian tradition. By contrast, the two youngest children, Ferdinand and Catherine, were born and raised in Spain.

At the time of King Ferdinand's death, Cisneros was at Alcalá. A letter from the royal secretary, Juan Ruiz de Calcena, informed him of his appointment as regent. The letter requested that he take the reins of government as soon as possible. Ferdinand had appointed the Cardinal (and the secretary emphasized: "him alone") because he had confidence in his upright character and his ability to maintain peace and order in the realm. The Cardinal's firm hand was now necessary, he said, "because so far there is uncertainty everywhere whom to obey and follow. And the Infante [Ferdinand] is here and also the Queen of Aragon [Germaine de Foix], who are unable to decide where to go and by what means. There are also the delegates and ambassadors; and precautions have to be taken with respect to Navarre and other parts, where problems will arise in your absence, for in truth there is no one to give instructions, and everyone speaks in his own interest" (Cart. Sec. 250).

The misgivings Ferdinand had expressed on his deathbed about Cisneros' social status were not without foundation. It proved difficult for Cisneros to hold his own against the nobility, as Gómez tells us: "Just as the power of the Spanish nobility often threatened the monarchs, so Cisneros had to make a determined effort to represent the majesty of the office he held and get the better of the pride and arrogance of our nobles. And a man who had no noble lineage and was not supported by numerous and illustrious members of a noble family, could not do so without displaying the greatest prudence, supreme courage, and an extraordinary greatness of mind" (*De rebus gestis*, 377). Indeed Cisneros' stature as a self-made man was pointed out and his authority called into question by the Condestable Iñigo de Velasco. The words attributed to him by Gómez characterize the attitude of the Castilian nobility. "The nobles had suffered enough slavery during Ferdinand's lifetime," the Condestable reportedly said. It was intolerable to take orders now from a "monk in a cowl" and a *homo novus* (*De rebus gestis*, 395). This sentiment is confirmed by Pietro Martire, who observed: "Spain does not like to obey those who are not Kings." Cisneros' rule was suffered with impatience. In Martire's view his mission was "to build and to be a patron of letters rather than to command" (Ep. 573).

In the event, however, Cisneros was able to come to terms with the most powerful nobles, among them the Condestable who represented the Velasco family, the Duque del Infantado who was the head of the Mendozas, and the Almirante who was the spokesman of the Enríquez family. In March 1516 Alonso Manrique, then resident at the Burgundian court, wrote admiringly of the Cardinal's shrewd maneuvers after Ferdinand's death: "He worked wonders: he made provisions to safeguard the borders and looked after external affairs and planned for all contingencies and furthermore allied himself with the grandees. Of this everyone here is informed" (Cart. Sec. 264).

The Cardinal's secretary, Jorge Varacaldo, confirmed in December 1516 that Cisneros had found a *modus vivendi* and a "great league and brotherhood with many assurances had been formed with the Cardinal" (Cart. Sec. 71–2).

Cisneros' liaison at the Burgundian court in the months following Ferdinand's death was Alonso Manrique de Lara, Bishop of Badajoz and later of Córdoba. Manrique's political fortunes were on the rise. Active on Prince Philip's behalf in the power struggle with Ferdinand, he was obliged to leave Spain for Burgundy, where he was rewarded for his efforts with a seat on the Council of Flanders. At the time of Ferdinand's death, he was Charles' chaplain. In March 1516 he wrote a confidential report to Cisneros concerning the situation at Charles' court. He advised the Cardinal to send a personal representative to Brussels, preferably "a jurist, old, prudent, experienced, and conscientious." The man sent by Cisneros was Diego López de Ayala, whose subsequent despatches paint a lively picture of the negotiations and intrigues that characterized the period between Ferdinand's death in 1516 and Charles' arrival in Spain the following year. Ayala was well connected. He belonged to the old Castilian aristocracy. His cousin Pedro López de Ayala was the third Conde de Fuensalida; another cousin held the post of ambassador at the English court. Little is known of Diego Ayala's life other than that he was a canon of Toledo and had translated a number of Italian authors (among them, Boccaccio) into Spanish. In 1508 he became Cisneros' Provisioner and Vicar general, that is, his chief administrator and right-hand man in Toledo, and looked after affairs in the Cardinal's absence. Unlike others at the court of Brussels, he made no effort to benefit personally from his new appointment. Indeed he wanted to set an example in what he saw as a mercenary court. His integrity was recognized by Cisneros, who praised him as a man of principles in a letter to Charles: "Be assured that he is a person of great nobility and comes from a long line of gentlemen, so that all his actions and words are straightforward" (Cart. Xim. 217).

Both of Cisneros' correspondents at the court of Brussels reported in some detail on the personal characteristics of the heir to the throne. Manrique described Charles as a talented young man "with good inclinations and natural greatness". Unfortunately, he wrote, "he speaks not a word of Spanish, and if he understands anything, it is very little. ... He is very much controlled [by others], and does and says nothing that is not suggested and told to him. He very much follows his council and is subject to it. We could wish that he would speak up and take charge in some form and would not leave his council to speak and act for him. After all he is almost 17 years old" (Cart. Sec., March 1516, pp. 254–5). In his letter Manrique also pointed out the principal powers at court: Jean Le Sauvage and Guillaume de Croÿ, Lord of Chièvres. Le Sauvage had made a stellar political career. He was appointed councillor in 1490, became Chancellor of Brabant in 1509, and Grand Chancellor of Burgundy in 1515. On Ferdinand's death he was appointed Chancellor of Castile *in absentia*. Guillaume de Croÿ, later Marquis of Aarschot, had been made Charles' chamberlain and mentor in 1509 and was the chief policy-maker after Charles had been declared of age in 1515. In his letter, Manrique noted that Chièvres was "a native Frenchman on both his father's and mother's side, ... he is much beholden to the King of France and writes to him often, saluting him as 'Your humble servant and vassal'" (Cart. Sec. 258). Chièvres was at the time involved in negotiations leading up to the Treaty of Noyon (1517) and was indeed the chief architect of the peace between France and Burgundy, securing the duchy's borders in preparation for Charles' departure for Spain. Chièvres' francophile policy was no doubt a matter of *Realpolitik*. Charles could not safely depart for Spain until the treaty with France was concluded. Manrique furthermore warned Cisneros that the Flemish court was controlled by money: "Greed rules among the people here, in all social classes, for however religious they are, greed is not considered a sin or an evil ... everything is bought and sold" (Cart. Sec. 255–6).

Charles' liaison with Cisneros was Adrian of Utrecht, the future Pope Adrian VI. Adrian, a theologian at the University of Louvain, had become Charles' tutor in 1507 and a member of his council in 1512. In October 1515 he had been sent to Spain to secure Ferdinand's agreement to Charles' succession. Martire describes his delicate negotiations with Ferdinand in some detail. The King had a personal bias in favour of his younger grandson, Ferdinand, but Adrian drew an attractive picture of Prince Charles as entirely devoted to his grandfather and obedient to his wishes. He prudently agreed to all conditions set by Ferdinand, knowing that they could be disregarded with impunity after his death.

For Cisneros the continued presence of Adrian in Spain was

awkward. It presented a certain challenge to his authority as regent. The Cardinal rested his authority on the legal argument that Isabel had made Ferdinand regent until Charles reached the age of twenty, and Ferdinand had appointed Cisneros his successor. "And above all, according to the laws of Spain and the customs of our forefathers, no foreigner — and Adrian was a Belgian — could be appointed" (Gómez, *De rebus gestis*, 379). He cooperated to a certain extent with Adrian, but according to one contemporary source the ambassador complained that he was *de facto* shut out from making decisions, "that he could do nothing, because the Cardinal was doing everything and did not let him share equitably in the task of governing" (Retana, *Cisneros*, 39). Ayala (Cart. Sec. 204–5) commented on the tug of war in January 1516. He advised Cisneros to keep control of the situation by lodging Adrian in his own palace and treating him with such marked honour that no one could allege that he was keeping him under surveillance. Indeed, letters from Charles to Cisneros indicate that Adrian was made Bishop of Tortosa and Inquisitor of Aragon on the Cardinal's request (Bergenroth, *Letters and Papers*, #23). It is significant, moreover, that Charles' letter ratifying Cisneros' position as regent refers to Adrian merely as his "ambassador" (Díaz-Plaja, *Historia de España*, 97).

Cisneros' authority as regent had been confirmed by Charles in a letter of 14 February 1516, in which he was given an exclusive mandate "to govern and administer justice in the Kingdom of Castile" in Charles' absence and asked to advise and counsel the heir to the throne, which counsel he promised to respect "as if I had received it from my father, for I see your good intentions and holy zeal in God's service and in ours, and for the universal good, justice and peace in our realms, and for all of Christendom" (Díaz-Plaja, *Historia de España*, 97). But Cisneros felt that he needed a more specific document giving him power to constitute tribunals, appoint corregidores and members of the Royal Council, and establish fiscal control. Accordingly, he directed Ayala, his agent at the Flemish court, to obtain from Charles plenary powers that would enable him to maintain peace and order: "Request from his Highness, now the King, to send me plenary power for the time until His Highness comes to these territories," he wrote on 3 April 1516 (Cart. Xim. 102). "And this power should cover all matters concerning the administration of justice and finance, and the authority, when necessary, to dismiss those holding office, whatever the office be, and replace them with others. Although this power will be used only when necessary and to keep up the pressure, it is important that this power be far-reaching and come by the first mail, for there are always arguments about authority." He was careful to avoid any semblance of personal ambition: "God knows, I have hesitated a great deal and for a long time to request this power. I hate nothing so much as making requests that smack of ambition, but it is required in the service of God and of His Highness and in the interest of peace in these realms."

The desired reply to Cisneros' request for plenipotentiary powers was given by Charles in a missive of 4 June 1516: "I send you the power to govern; it was not done earlier because it seemed that the previous provision was sufficient; considering your person, dignity, knowledge, spirit, prudence, and life, any power I give you is small. I entrust and recommend to your care the state and conscience of my lady the Queen and of myself, our honour, justice, peace, and the kingdom" (Retana, *Cisneros*, 104).

Queen Juana and the Royal Title

In spite of the censored version of Ferdinand's will and its implication that Charles was not to come into his grandparents' heritage until a future date, the young prince almost immediately claimed for himself the title of "King", disregarding the protests of the Royal Council that this was inappropriate during his mother's lifetime. They despatched a letter to Charles, remonstrating with him: "In our opinion Your Highness should not take this step. It is not in accordance with divine or secular law. Your Highness is in peaceful possession of this kingdom; no one denies that it is yours to govern henceforth as you please and give orders high and low, so that there is no need to use the title of King during the lifetime of our lady, the Queen" (Retana, *Cisneros*, 92–3). This opinion is also reflected in a letter from Martire to Marliano, one of Charles' privy councillors: "He is of course the heir. Everyone admits that. But they say it is not customary to give the title of King to anyone while the holder of that title is still alive ... You will say, but he governs on behalf of his mother, who is ill. This, too, the people grant, but they say he may do so with the legitimate title of Prince. To avoid unpopularity [Ferdinand] relinquished the title of King of Castile on the death of his wife, since it was not his by right. You would make the young man unpopular if you, who are entrusted with his education, would act in this manner. ... [The Aragonese] say they will deny authorization, if it is requested from them" (Ep. 568). It appears, however, that Charles was fond of the royal title and was not discouraged by his advisors from usurping it. The Bishop of Badajoz reported to Cisneros: "He smiles and is pleased when they call him King. It's the same with the title Emperor. He puts 'King of the Romans' in his letters and signs in this fashion, but everyone calls him and writes to him by the title 'Emperor' " (Cart. Sec. 264). In the end the Council under Cisneros acquiesced and issued the necessary proclamation. There was no adverse reaction from the people, as had been feared. Cisneros reported to Diego López de Ayala, his deputy at the Flemish court, that the proclamation on 12 April 1516 was duly celebrated in Toledo and Madrid and greeted with shouts (unprompted, Cisneros insisted) of "Castile, Castile! For the Queen and King Charles, our lords" (Cart. Xim. 109).

In the meantime, Queen Juana's condition had worsened. She refused to leave her room, insisted on sleeping on the floor rather than in her bed, rejected warm clothes to protect her against the cold, and let "her dinner rot, so that there was a repugnant smell about" (Gómez, *De rebus gestis*, 429). The only company she appreciated was that of her cats, who did not return her affection. Her face was reportedly disfigured with scratches. The Queen had been for some years in the care of the *corregidor* of Toledo, Mosen Luis Ferrer. Cisneros now recommended to Charles that he be removed from the post. Ferrer protested the dismissal. In his letter to Cisneros he confirmed that the Queen had been ill treated, but declined responsibility. He had merely been following orders. His enemies had maligned him, saying that it was his fault "that the Queen our Lady was not restored to health, and that she had been a prisoner while the King her father lived ... I see from Your Lordship's orders, you believe their tales, and think that I am as they depict me. Your Lordship has amidst your great occupations forgotten to consider that so wise a King and one whom Your Lordship knew and loved so much, would not have shown me such confidence if I really were so evil ... But if God created her such as she is, it is impossible to effect more than His Divine Majesty permits and vouchsafes, and the King her father could never do more until, to prevent her from destroying herself by refusing to eat if she did not get her will, he had to give orders that force be applied to preserve her life. Was that my fault? It was not in my hands nor in my power to avoid it" (Bergenroth, *Letters and Papers*, Supplement vol. II, #23). Ferrer's protests were of no avail. By September 1516 he had been relieved of his responsibilities, as Cisneros' letter to the King indicates. "Concerning the guard for our Lady the Queen, your mother, the situation has been remedied and is now well in hand ... I have sent in [Ferrer's] place a gentleman by name of Hernan Duque d'Estrada, who has long been in charge of important affairs and since he is a prudent and experienced man, she is in good hands" (Cart. Xim. 144–5). According to Gómez, the new governor of the Queen's household showed great sensitivity in his treatment of Juana and persuaded the disturbed woman to adopt healthier practices and "abandon the difficult and inhuman life" she had led so far (*De rebus gestis*, 429). Cisneros' secretary, Jorge Varacaldo, is more matter-of-fact in accounting for the changing of the guards: the Duke was "a good man and deserved a favour" (Cart. Sec. Ep. 20).

The Cardinal's Militia

An anecdote related by Gómez de Castro reflects the politically volatile situation encountered by Cisneros. Asked to show his letters of authorization, Cisneros paraded his armed guard and told his challengers "to communicate to their followers that he had received no other authorization from Charles than the one they had seen themselves" (*De rebus gestis*, 396–7). The story, although apocryphal, shows Cisneros' determination. Faced with the threat of revolt, he resorted to organizing a citizen militia. His initiative was immediately denounced as being, not a security measure, but a covert move against the nobility and an effort to build up his personal rule. Whatever Cisneros' motives, his actions were of questionable legality since he had proceeded without awaiting Charles' approval of his plan. Royal assent was given eventually, however (letter of 30 April, quoted by Retana, *Cisneros*, II: 155). Recruits were attracted by special privileges and tax exemptions in return for voluntary service. A report by General Gil Rengifo sets out the incentives and penalties for members of the militia (Retana, *Cisneros*, II:158–9): They were to be rewarded with pay in advance, tax advantages, exemption from local jurisdiction for the duration of the campaign, and the right to bear arms. When setting out for a campaign, they were to "go to confession and communion and swear the following oath: to serve Your Highness well and loyally; to guard the churches, which contain the Holy Sacrament, against robbery and dishonest acts ... to guard the honour of women ... to die with their comrades in arms and let no danger make turncoats of them. If they desert, their comrades must kill them" (quoted by Retana, *Cisneros*, II:158). Cisneros' biographer, Gómez de Castro, praised the moral advantages of offering employment of this sort: "Young men, if they are not employed in honest ways, dissipate their life with pleasures, which are more dangerous than arms." Military training, by contrast, was a most useful occupation. "With organized militias such as these, powerful nations have been defeated" (*De rebus gestis*, 402). More concretely, "the formation of this militia meant trouble for the seditious element that was fond of upheaval. It did away with opportunities to instigate revolt and uprisings; and with the organization of the militia disappeared the licence they took during the absence of the King" (ibid., 403).

Cisneros recruited men between the ages of twenty and forty and supplied them with arms. The bailiff (*alguacil*) of the town served as the captain of the troop, supervised their training on the first Sunday of every month, and was their paymaster. The reponse to Cisneros' recruiting efforts was overwhelming. By September 1516 he had a troop of more than 30,000 men; and he maintained the militia in the face of considerable resistance from the nobility, who regarded his action an infringement on their privileges, and of towns who found the militia troublesome and sometimes paid not to have them within their walls. They lodged complaints at Charles' court, but Cisneros defended his initiative (letter from Varacaldo to Ayala, 14 Oct. 1516): "The militia does not cost the King one *maravedi*. They are local people and of modest means. There are captains in each city to train them well in matters of ordinance and to drill them each week, and there are few ruffians and criminals among them ... They will protect justice, make the King powerful, both inside the realm and outside, and in all the world" (Cart. Sec. 39–40; cf. also p. 76). The argument was repeated in another urgent letter to Ayala: "Tell the King that he ought to give [Cisneros] freedom to act and that he must not listen to talk. [Cisneros] knows more about the realm than the rest and has the best intentions. We are surprised that in his letter he gave instruction to disband the armed troop. We cannot understand how that can be, for if the troops now in Castile are disbanded, it won't be long before the whole kingdom is ablaze" (Cart. Sec. 53; cf. Cart. Xim. 169–70). Similar cautions appear also in letters written in September and October 1516. The Cardinal warned Charles to beware of the nobility, insisted that the recruits in the militia were honest men, and emphasized that they did not burden the King financially. Cisneros' arguments failed to win the day, however. An investigation by Charles' emissary, Charles de la Chaulx, sent to Spain in December, resulted in recruiting being suspended. The following October Cisneros was still recommending his troop to the King. The mercenaries now stationed in Italy were expensive to maintain and "commit crimes and acts of robbery wherever they are." It would be better to deploy the militia of 25,000 honest men, "who are not practiced criminals and if they do anything illegal can be punished and cost nothing until the day they are called up to serve" (Cart. Xim. 257).

In his chronicle of Charles' reign, Pero Mexía offers this evaluation of Cisneros' project: "The Cardinal-regent regarded it useful for the defense of the realm to have an armed corps of able and trained men. He ordered that each city, town, and settlement in Castile have a certain number of infantry and cavalry, ... to whom he conceded certain tax exemptions, privileges, and other honours. At first this was regarded by many as good instruction and government, but afterwards there were reports to the contrary and many disadvantages ensued. Tumult and discontent arose because some did not have the arms the authorities were obliged to provide, others walked around armed, left their work and assignments to do drills and exercises, and ... committed crimes." For this reason cities such as Salamanca, Burgos, Leon, and Valladolid refused to comply with the order. "And so the new order never had any beneficial effect or was not reinforced, and afterwards, when the King's arrival was imminent, it was decided that this kind of militia served no purpose and it was disbanded" (Mexía, *Cronica*, 74).

External Threats: Navarre, North Africa, Sicily

Cisneros had to deal, not only with resistance from within, but also with external threats to peace. Navarre had been annexed to Castile in 1515, but now Jean d'Albret, who had been dispossessed, saw his chance to recapture his position. The matter had been drawn to

Cisneros' attention by Charles who, in confirming his regency, had instructed him to ensure peace in the kingdom of Navarre: "We commission you to make the necessary provisions and take measures, as you see fit and serves our best interest and ensures the pacification and security of the said kingdom" (Cart. Sec. 226). Cisneros, well aware of the dangerous situation in Navarre, attempted a negotiated settlement, as letters exchanged between the two parties show. Jean d'Albret, however, decided on the military option and invaded Navarre in March 1516, supported by a French troop. He found the border fortress, San Juan de Pie del Puerto, well defended. The small garrison there was, moreover, reinforced by a Spanish force under Fernando de Villalba. Martire gives a dramatic account of their forced march: "They crossed the Pyrenees by difficult paths, through deep ravines and along steep banks that were barely passable. They were up to their knees in snow and had practically nothing to eat. Nevertheless they overcame all obstacles and suffered all hardship. Without boots, treading on thorns and pointed rocks covered with snow, with their leggings and soldier's cloaks torn, they advanced toward the enemy in forced marches" (Cart. Xim. 101). D'Albret was forced to retreat and died a few months later. To secure the region Cisneros ordered a number of fortifications razed, reasoning that they might fall into enemy hands (Cart. Xim. 109). At the same time, D'Albret's sympathizers were removed from key positions in Navarre and deported. Cisneros nominated Antonio Manrique de Lara y Castro, the Duke of Najera, to the position of viceroy and saw his candidate confirmed by Charles.

Cisneros then turned his attention to securing the southern coast of Spain and defending her influence in North Africa. Spanish possessions were threatened by the pirate Chair-ed-Din (Barbarossa). His attack on Bougie was fought off with difficulty; the king of Tenes suffered death at his hands, and his heirs turned for support to Spain. On 25 April 1516 Cisneros sent news to Brussels that Algiers had been taken: "A Turkish pirate called Barbarossa appeared in Algiers and through plots and treason captured the place. This has caused great discord and dissension among the Moors themselves, which is bound to lead to their ruin" (Cart. Xim. 112).

Spanish plans to recoup Algiers and deal a blow to Barbarossa had appeared successful at first. An encounter between Spanish and Turkish ships at Alicante ended in victory for the former. Ruiz reported jubilantly that "our men destroyed the whole armada of the enemy and killed four hundred and took prisoners, although only a few, for they defended themselves with determination, preferring to die rather than be taken prisoners ... and we know that they were on their way to bring relief to Algiers" (Cart. Xim. 126). Cisneros had allotted funds to the maintainance and expansion of the fleet, an expenditure unpopular with the court of Brussels, and now hoped that this victory would justify his military policy in Charles' eyes. "His Highness will see what advantage came of repairing and equipping the galleys," he wrote (ibid.).

Diego de Vera, whom Cisneros had put in charge of the operation, appears to have been a poor choice, however. Pietro Martire reported on the situation to Marliani: "Barbarossa has used the same astute arguments that Mohammed once used against the Romans. He has convinced the people [of Bougie and Algiers] to abandon the Christian faith, saying it was unjust that the blessed and saintly followers of Mohammed should obey and be subject to Christians, the enemies of their religion. He promises, if they make him their King, to free them (in accordance with the Moslem law) of the yoke of the Christians and guarantee their safety. ... On being informed of this, our Cardinal-regent assembled an army of some eight thousand soldiers, who are now ready for the campaign. I shall make no predictions about the outcome of this venture. In my opinion, he has not chosen a general who is capable of leading this expedition. It is a certain Diego de Vera, a captain of the artillery. May God bless his venture. The man is more blustering and vainglorious than brave" (Ep. 574, July 1516). Vera's personal qualities may have been a factor in the subsequent failure of the campaign, but there were other contributing factors. He had difficulties obtaining the necessary provisions and he set out with a poorly equipped and manned fleet. According to Mosen Quint, the *alcalde* of Peñon del Argel, the crew consisted of "monks and farmhands, who had never carried arms." The expedition went ahead on 29 September, with disastrous results. In the battle with Barbarossa some 3000 Spaniards were killed, but the impact of the unfortunate campaign was minimized in official correspondence. In October Cisneros' secretary, Jorge Varacaldo, wrote to Ayala, asking him to control rumours: "His Majesty must be advised ... that Diego de Vera went to Algiers, as we informed His Majesty, and since the Turks there had had advance warning, they obtained assistance from their allies and relatives and neighbours, so that they could not have been better prepared. Diego de Vera was a little careless in putting a few people ashore and suffered some reverses. Some were killed, but fewer than reported, and he was on the point of correcting the situation. It was a small matter and deserved no attention. Our information is unconfirmed, but even assuming that something [adverse] happened, it is nothing much, and those who bear us a grudge could magnify it at will" (Cart. Sec. 41–2). Cisneros himself wrote to Ayala that "the business of Algiers was much less significant than they would have you believe, for the number of prisoners and dead did not exceed one thousand, and the cause of the loss was the greed and disorganization of the infantry." The footsoldiers were "vagabonds and wretches, fugitives from justice and criminals, who wherever they go commit a thousand robberies in the villages through which they pass." He took the opportunity once again to recommend his militia, whose recruits were honest men and respecters of the law (Cart. Xim. 186–7).

Cisneros also revived plans of a crusade in the Eastern Mediterranean. In the summer of 1516 he sought a renewal of the papal privilege allowing the collection of a *cruzada*, a crusade tax. This system of selling indulgences to finance military action against infidels had developed into a regular crown revenue and was exacted with unwarranted severity. The Castilian *cortes* of 1512 described the extortion practised by the preachers: "They keep men two or three days in the churches from morning to evening and oblige the people to listen to their sermons. Thus they prevent them from earning their daily bread; and when they find that they cannot induce them to accept the said [papal] Bull, they parade through the streets, asking everyone they meet if they know their Our Father and Hail Mary; and if by chance they find anyone who does not, they force him to accept the said Bull as a penance; and if any one fails to do so, they drag him along in shackles, making him listen to their preachings, and thus force him at last by compulsion and intimidation to do their will" (quoted by Merriman, *Spanish Empire*, II: 132–3).

Cisneros was keen on having the papal privilege renewed in order to finance the planned campaign in the Mediterranean. He noted in October 1516 that France had obtained preferential treatment (he was referring to the Concordat of Bologna), whereas he was still waiting for permission to collect the crusade tax (Cart. Xim. 165). In

December he returned to this subject: "The King of France has been given the right to make church appointments and to levy crusade tax even though he has never fought a war against the infidels as did Spain, and has never shed blood for the faith" (Cart. Xim. 185). It was only in response to his protests that Pope Leo X promised, in a brief of December 1516, to renew the privilege of the Spanish Crown. Negotiations with the pope continued during spring of 1517. The minutes of a memorandum written by Cisneros in March 1517 read: "In view of the great damage that has been and is being done by the Turks and other infidels in the maritime areas of Spain and in other realms, to the detriment of Your Highness [Charles] and Christendom, and desiring a remedy, it is my opinion that they cannot be remedied in any other way but by requesting the crusade tax from the Holy Father ... and since His Holiness saw that this was necessary he wrote to me a brief in which he effectively conceded the said crusade tax" (Cart. Xim. 264-5). But he could not proceed without a bull officially granting him the privilege of levying the tax. This was not the only factor causing a delay. It was also necessary to wait for Charles' arrival in Spain, for only then could matters be expedited. At present, he said in a candid letter to his secretary Varacaldo, the motivation was lacking. "Even if the [bull granting the] crusade tax arrives — if His Highness does not come to his realm, what has been done will be of little benefit, for those who must serve in such expeditions, want to put their king and lord under obligation and be rewarded for their labour with prizes and titles" (Cart. Xim. 270).

During Cisneros' regency troubles also erupted in Sicily, where the people rose in revolt against the unpopular viceroy, Hugo de Moncada. Pero Mexía describes the circumstances: "When the people of the city of Palermo heard that the Catholic King had died, they claimed that the power of the viceroy had lapsed with his death. They refused obedience and discussed the appointment of governors. Certain counts and barons hostile toward Moncada because he had brought them to justice were reportedly the moving force behind the rebellion" (Mexía, *Cronica*, 69). They incited the people to storm the Palace of the Inquisition and attack the viceroy's seaside mansion. According to Pietro Martire, the rebel's fury was directed at Moncada personally. In the end, Moncada accepted the inevitable and departed for Naples. Cisneros first reported on the situation in Sicily in a letter of 25 April 1516 (Cart. Xim. 112). In August and in December he advised once again that "Naples and Sicily are in great danger" (Cart. Xim. 127, 186). In Naples the viceroy Ramon de Cardona was able to maintain control; the Sicilian uprising was contained with difficulty. In 1518 Charles replaced Moncada with Hector Pignatelli, Count of Monteleone. Thereafter an uneasy peace prevailed.

7 *The Final Months*

Much of the information on the diplomatic whirl preceding Charles' arrival comes from letters exchanged between Cisneros' representative in Brussels, Diego López de Ayala, and the two men who looked after Cisneros' correspondence: the jurist Jorge Varacaldo and Francisco Ruiz, Bishop of Avila. Ruiz, a native of Toledo, had entered Cisneros' service when he was a young man of eighteen, as has been mentioned. He became his confidant and was a loyal follower, but lacked sophistication and displayed little talent for diplomacy. The letters he sent to Ayala during the frequent illnesses of the Cardinal are written in a crude style and contain many colloquialisms. He was, moreover, unrealistic in his estimate of Cisneros' power and correspondingly insensitive to the power play at the Burgundian court.

The jurist Jorge Varacaldo, by contrast, was entirely realistic. He had been in Cisneros' service since 1509, and in January 1516 was despatched to Brussels for two months as the Cardinal's personal emissary (Cart. Xim. 196). While not disloyal to the Cardinal, he kept a sharp lookout for his own interests. The Cardinal had appointed him Secretary of the Military Orders, but the appointment needed royal assent, and he frequently importuned Ayala to obtain ratification of the document. He finally achieved his object, but his pleasure was short-lived. The King reversed his position, as a letter from Cisneros to Ayala indicates. "You knew how to obtain for Secretary Varacaldo the secretaryship of the Orders of Santiago, Calatrava, and Alcántara in the name of His Highness," he wrote. "... I have now been told that His Highness had not been well informed about this matter and wishes to appoint another person to this office. Since the change is not in his interest and no one but the said secretary should have the post, you must speak about it to His Highness" (Cart. Xim. 120). Nothing could be done, however, and Varacaldo had to relinquish the post.

Letters exchanged between Cisneros and representatives at the court in Brussels show that the question of his own authority remained on the agenda. Cisneros felt that he must have more discretion over patronage appointments, for "to have the authority to take away but not to give is the devil of a job and makes him enemies everywhere," Varacaldo wrote candidly (Cart. Sec. 44) in October 1516. He returned to this subject in another letter to Ayala, asking him to make clear to Charles that Cisneros had "to govern and satisfy many people, so that it is imperative that he give them something and to bestow favours on them or else he cannot but encounter difficulties" (Cart. Sec. 56).

The appointment of foreigners or expatriates to prestigious positions created much resentment. The general opinion was that Spanish wealth was being funnelled into foreign coffers, as decisions were being made by an absentee court. Many complained of Charles' advisors at the Burgundian court, Martire wrote. "It is unjust that the affairs of Spain should be subject to the dictates of the Flemish in the North. Their mentality and upbringing is very different from the Spanish custom" (Ep. 580). Widespread corruption was alleged. Cisneros' secretary requested Ayala to discuss the matter of patronage appointments for courtiers in Brussels: "Let those gentlemen protect their honour. The custom in Spain is different from the custom in Flanders. Here we do not allow that anyone does things other than in a clean-cut fashion and as they ought to be done" (Cart. Sec. 18). Alonso Manrique, another of Cisneros' correspondents, confirmed that the Burgundian court was rife with corruption. He used the occasion to assure the Cardinal of his own integrity. He had deliberately refrained from asking any favour for himself, to demonstrate that not all Spaniards were self-seeking (Cart. Sec. 269).

Conversely, Cisneros was accused at the court in Brussels of acting from motives of personal ambition and without regard for Charles' interests. Adrian of Utrecht appears to have been one of the accusers. The Cardinal asked Ayala to counter his allegations and convince Charles that he was the King's greatest asset in Spain (Cart. Sec. 19). Ruiz wrote in a similar vein, defending his patron in a letter to Charles, but it appears that Ayala, whom he used as go-between, did not think it advisable to convey Ruiz' outspoken letter to the King. Reacting to allegations that Cisneros had been critical of the Burgundian court and was not acting in good faith, Ruiz wrote:

If Your Highness knew the work that is being done in your interest, you would have given instruction to write us a friendlier letter than this one, to give strength and courage to your servants to undertake such great burdens, especially to myself, because with all the illness that afflicted the Cardinal, the greater part of the labour rested on my shoulders, and the labour is so great that since the death of the Catholic King of blessed memory, the Cardinal and I have each been sick twice and we expect to die in this labour, unless Your Highness rescues us with his hoped-for arrival ... let it be known to Your Highness who are your true servants ... [Far from acting in bad faith], we have, because of our loyalty and services to Your Highness, made enemies of the people in many ways, both here and there [in Burgundy], because we do not wish to do anything for them that is a disservice to God and Your Highness ... [Cisneros' enemies] frequently visited the ambassador [Adrian]. We have no suspicions of him — he is a person of integrity and of angelic character — but under the pretext that it is for the good and in the service of Your Highness, these people make him [Adrian] write some of those things, for the purpose I have indicated, and they blame it all on me, because, as I have said, they don't dare to blame the Cardinal. (Cart. Sec. 23-4)

In August 1516, when the Cardinal was still entertaining hopes that Charles would arrive in Spain later that year, he begged the King to delay making further appointments until that date. "For at that time Your Highness will be able to obtain information of what needs to be done and who is best suited for the said offices. It would be in your interest not to make provisions about anything and to make no promises of any kind until you are here in your kingdoms. You will be able to make much better decisions concerning everything after some consultation and deliberation. And as soon as a decision has been made regarding your journey, it is imperative that you take care to advise me of it, for I intend to go to Burgos to join Your Highness on your disembarkation" (Cart. Xim. 130).

Charles' journey was delayed for another year, however, while negotiations with France continued in an effort to secure the borders of the Netherlands during his absence. The treaty of Noyon, which provided the guarantees needed for Charles' departure, was concluded too late in the year to allow him to set out. His departure accordingly had to be delayed until the next spring. In the meantime, two new representatives arrived from the Burgundian court: Amerstorff and La Chaulx. The latter may have come in the capacity of a judge (cf. Cart. Xim. 183). Pero Mexía speaks of his mission in vague terms. He was to "explain the reasons for the delay in Charles' departure and other important matters" (Mexía, *Crónica*, 78). Cisneros was naturally protective of his powers, which he did not wish to see curtailed by the King's delegates. A diplomatic war ensued about points of etiquette. Cisneros refused to pay La Chaulx the courtesy of riding out to meet him on his arrival; on seeing his signature on official documents, he had them torn up and rewritten over his own signature. On Cisneros' instructions, his secretary, Varacaldo, protested inroads on the Cardinal's authority: "According to the instructions sent to the ambassador [Adrian]," he noted defensively, "all matters pertaining to jurisdiction have been left in the Cardinal's hands. The matter of appointing judges [La Chaulx?] is an important one. I cannot understand that they would not realize the inappropriateness of this new development" (7 Dec. 1516, Ep. 16, Cart. Sec. 91). According to Gómez, the Cardinal himself wrote to Charles outlining his position: "Only he, and no Belgian, nor indeed the King himself until he reached majority, had the right to appoint judges in the royal tribunals, ... city prefects, treasury officials [etc]; ... and it was he whose business it was to look after the garrisons and their prefects ... and the ministers in the Privy Council" (*De rebus gestis*, 470). Not surprisingly, the Burgundians judged that Cisneros "had written with great clarity but not enough prudence and astuteness" (471). A follow-up letter written in the name of Cisneros and the Royal Council was more respectful but once again requested in so many words that important offices not be entrusted to foreigners. The request was couched in diplomatic terms: "In former days no one was entrusted with more elevated tasks unless he had previously passed through lower offices and given proof of his valour and integrity" (475). Burgundians continued to enjoy the King's favour, however, and receive important posts, to the frustration of the Spanish nobles, who accused the foreigners of despoiling their country.

In 1517 Cisneros saw his competitor for the governmental authority, Adrian of Utrecht, elevated to the cardinalate. He had been aware of the plan for some time, but did not know the details. In October 1516, he asked Ayala to investigate a rumour concerning negotiations with the Pope that "someone be made cardinal this Christmas on Charles' request. But we do not know for whom he requests the honour." He instructed Ayala to pursue the matter and see "that it be delayed and that nothing more be said of it until the King comes to this realm" (Cart. Sec. 43–4). Adrian was one of thirty-one cardinals created by Leo X in June 1517, an act that generated much ill will. Reform-minded Christians everywhere deplored the appointments as simoniacal and cheapening the dignity of the office. Martire's reaction was typical. He took a dim view of the events: "The Pope has ... created thirty-one cardinals in one month, going against the opinion of the incumbent cardinals. Everyone is biting their lips in anger. The general opinion is that it was done to collect money. The status of the cardinals has been lowered" (Ep. 596). Cisneros shared Martire's feelings about the wholesale appointments, but his specific objection was, no doubt, to yet another patronage appointment for a non-Spaniard.

In the meantime preparations for Charles' departure for Spain began in earnest. On 7 September the royal party embarked on the journey. While Cisneros was making preparations to meet Charles, he fell ill. There were rumours that he had been poisoned. Gómez reports that the Cardinal received a warning not to eat trout prepared for him because it contained a powerful poison. Cisneros, however, ignored the warning. The person who served and pretasted the trout was reported to have taken ill as well. Martire offers a less sensational explanation for Cisneros' illness: old age and the raw climate of northern Spain. "He was born and raised in the protected southern part of the mountains of Segovia. The northern air harms him quite a bit. The physicians predict that his days are numbered. He is more than eighty years old" (Ep. 598). Cisneros recovered, however, and set out to meet the king.

On 19 September 1517 the royal fleet reached the coast of Spain. Charles and his retinue made an unplanned landing at Villaviciosa between Gijon and Santander. Martire tells us that they were caught in a violent storm and driven off course. Charles and his sister Eleanor reportedly weathered the situation, but the rest suffered from seasickness. There were anxious moments, moreover, when the royal party was given what appeared to be a hostile reception:

When the people [of Villaviciosa] saw an unknown fleet approach, they assumed that it was a French maneuver. They hurriedly took up arms and evacuated the women, children, and old people to the safety of the mountains. Everyone capable of bearing arms … occupied the hills looking out on the sea and they took their stand determined to offer resistance. A fair spectacle! From the royal ship a cry arose: Spain! Spain! Our Catholic King, our King! When they heard the cry, they dropped [their weapons] … Unarmed, they thronged the beach. They saluted the King with all due respect and fetched back their families and household goods from the mountains. With apparent signs of joy they received the King into their midst. (Ep. 599)

Charles and his retinue now proceeded inland toward Valladolid. The Cardinal's health was still precarious, but he advanced to meet the King. As soon as he was informed of the King's arrival, moreover, he took measures to dispatch Prince Ferdinand to the Netherlands.

Cisneros and the Infante Ferdinand

In the wake of King Ferdinand's death there had been concern that rebellious nobles would seize on Charles' younger brother, Ferdinand, as their pretender. At the time Cisneros preempted any such action by having the Infante brought to Castile and keeping him under close supervision. In a letter to Ayala the Cardinal describes the situation (Cart. Xim. 62, p. 104): "After the death of the Catholic King I went to Guadalupe with the sole purpose of looking after the affairs of Prince Ferdinand and to avoid revolts and upheavals in the realm such as occurred at other times in like situations. And afterwards I did not risk being apart from him for one single day." His purpose was to minimize the risk of plotting. He feared that the fourteen-year-old prince, disappointed by the provisions of his grandfather's will, would be open to suggestions of asserting his claims to Aragon. He therefore advised Charles to "appoint two persons to take charge of the Infante — trusted men, for those in charge now are not at all suitable" (Cart. Xim. 104). He was referring to Ferdinand's guardian, the Commendador Mayor Pedro Núñes de Guzmán, and his tutor, the Dominican Alvaro Osorio, bishop of Astorga. By April 1517 Cisneros was convinced that there was a conspiracy among Aragonese nobles favouring the succession of Prince Ferdinand. In September Ayala was requested to inform Charles that a "diabolical" plot had been discovered, whose instigator was the Bishop of Astorga (Cart. Sec. 151). Cisneros himself wrote to ask again that the Prince's retinue be dismissed and his guardians be replaced with "two men who are not from Spain" (Cart. Xim. 154, Sept. 1516). It was advisable to remove the Prince from the country, he said, but not until Charles himself had arrived. The following month he again asked for directions in this matter. At the same time the Bishop of Astorga departed for Brussels, "supposedly to take care of matters concerning the Infante entrusted to him by the Catholic King," as Varacaldo reported. He requested Ayala to watch the Bishop closely: "He is the most devious and unmanageable creature ever born, a master of evil arts and evil tongue and, so help me God, I fear if he obtains access to our liege, the King, he will poison him" (Cart. Sec. 60). In October Varacaldo wrote another letter to Ayala, requesting him to remind the King of the urgency of the situation. "As far as the business of the Infante is concerned," he wrote in code, "His Majesty must act, for it is more necessary than ever. Make sure that there is no delay about this, but the King must make every effort to come [to Spain]" (Cart. Sec. 41). He offered to give the King proof of the conspiracy on his arrival.

Shortly thereafter Cisneros took action, dismissing and replacing Ferdinand's retainers. The move came as a surprise to many. Obviously the plans had been well concealed. The young prince, who had formed strong attachments to some members of his retinue, was shaken. He remonstrated with Cisneros, but the cardinal persisted in his plans, which he said originated with Charles. An awkward interview took place:

> Ferdinand, almost crying, complained to Cisneros that he, whom he thought to be his friend, was treating him badly by depriving him, for no reason, of his attendants, who had been with him for a long time and were good and loyal men. ... Cisneros tried to calm the anxious prince with friendly words and promises of great things and a high position at the court of his brother, if he showed himself obedient ... Cisneros' words had no effect and did not convince the prince, and he replied: "So far I have experienced your love toward me, but now that I need it most I don't know where it has flown to. You have decided to ruin me and my friends, although you could help us. I have to find means to ensure that they come to no harm." At this Cisneros

was vexed and said somewhat more harshly: "Do as you please, Ferdinand, but I swear to you on your brother's head that, even if all of Spain worked against it, the orders of the King must be executed before tomorrow evening, and you more than anyone else must obey him."

This is the account given by Gómez. Martire, too, related the events in a letter dated 15 September 1517, concluding: "The whole Court was astounded by this sudden change. The cause is still unknown" (Ep. 600).

Although Gómez' dramatic version details a personal encounter between Ferdinand and the Cardinal, it was in fact Francisco Ruiz who took charge of the matter on behalf of his ailing master. Taking pride in his personal involvement he asked Ayala to report to the King: "I have fulfilled the royal command to dismiss the Commendador Mayor and the Bishop of Astorga and Gonzálo de Guzmán from the company of the Infante. The Cardinal was, as I said, indisposed, but I acted with such great diligence that the matter was transacted within a day. The whole world was astonished at such daring. Since His Highness at present has no other heir or successor but [Ferdinand], no one dared to do what we did, and to displease him in this manner; especially since people, for the most part, thought that His Highness would not come [to Spain]." Even after it was known that the royal party had embarked, there was speculation that they might perish at sea and fate might play into the hands of Ferdinand. He indicated, moreover, that he faced opposition from Adrian of Utrecht. "The Dean of Tortosa [Adrian] gave us so much trouble . . . for he and they were very close, so that not much was missing and the whole realm would have risen in rebellion, and the fact is that all correspondence came to him [Adrian] and, without saying anything to the Cardinal, he opened it, and then advised the Infante of everything . . . We entrusted the Infante to the Marques de Aguilar . . . and may it please His Highness not to make any changes . . . and tell Your Highness that in [the Cardinal's] opinion he should under no circumstances admit the Infante to his presence, for if they are together, it could happen that they destroy each other, for as soon as he has access to him, he will beg him to do what would give the whole realm much satisfaction, that is, not to send him away, poor and hopeless as he was. But in that respect he suffers no hardship, since our liege has given him a rich inheritance and will give him more" (Cart. Sec. 137–9). On 20 October Ruiz reported to Ayala that the Prince had resigned himself to the facts and made the best of the situation. "To show that he was complying with the wishes of our liege the King in all things, he dismissed twenty-seven persons who had been put at his service by the men who used to take care of him. His Highness ought to write him a gracious letter to thank him for everything" (Cart. Sec. 172).

The question has been raised whether Cisneros dismissed Ferdinand's retinue on his own authority or on orders from Charles. Much of the evidence points to the conclusion that he was acting on instruction. Ruiz at any rate refers (in the letter just quoted) to a "royal injunction" (*rreal mandamiento*). Instructions to this effect are not extant but are cited by Cisneros' biographer Gómez and by Pero Mexía in his *Crónica* ("ansi lo embio a mandar el Rey," p. 82). Finally there is a letter from Charles praising Cisneros' course of action: "As you know, I have written to the Most Illustrious Prince Ferdinand, my dear and much beloved brother, that I consider your actions well done" (quoted by Retana, *Cisneros*, II: 388). No doubt Ferdinand was a political liability and was dispatched to the Netherlands on Charles' arrival in Spain "for the greater peace of Castile," as Mexía explained (*Crónica*, 82).

Charles' Inland Journey

Charles' first concern was to proceed to Tordesillas and meet his mother, whom he had not seen for eleven years. Ruiz suggested that her state of mind was such that "Charles could well be pardoned for not paying her this courtesy visit" (153). The visit was not merely a matter of courtesy, however. Protocol, and indeed reasons of state, demanded that Charles meet with his mother to procure for himself the authorization to assume royal power. The meeting went well, as Pietro Martire reported: "The Queen put on clean clothes, which she rarely does, because she thinks that widowhood must manifest itself in a dirty appearance. And on her own initiative she gave them [Charles and his sister Eleanor] presents. But she has not the least concern for her realm. It's all the same to her whether Spain is ruined or prospers" (Ep. 602).

The next step was to meet with Cisneros and to hold *cortes* to formally receive their oath of fealty. Valladolid was the most suitable meeting place, as Cisneros informed the King. It offered a healthy location and had the necessary facilities to provide food and lodging for so large a gathering (Cart. Xim. 222). The Cardinal himself had advanced as far as Aranda, but poor health impeded further progress. Because of rumours of an outbreak of the plague he took refuge in the nearby Monastery of Aguilera. There was fear also for the health of the royal party and talk of moving the *cortes* to Segovia or even Toledo. In the meantime the members of the Regency Council had been chafing at the bit. Cisneros complained in a letter of 28 September that they had defied orders: "Your Highness wrote that the Infante and the ambassador and the council and the whole court should remain where they are and not move until Your Highness has sent instructions on where we were to meet His Majesty. ... The members of the council ignored this and left Aranda and advanced to a place some five leagues from here and have ruined the business of the suppliers of this court. It is unbelievable that the members of the council would dare shamelessly to disobey the command of Your Highness" (Cart. Xim. 225). Apparently the king supported Cisneros and rebuked the council for its insubordination. They returned to Aranda and sent a letter of apology to the Cardinal (Cart. Sec. 150).

In October Cisneros was still holding on to his authority as regent. Ruiz informed an unidentified addressee that Charles "did not intend to make any decisions until he had met [with Cisneros] ... it was not at all in the interest of [the King] to act until he had seen the Cardinal, for he will inform him of everything and give him an account of all persons and tell him everything that concerns the interests of his realm" (Cart. Xim. 256). By the end of the month the Cardinal's health had taken a turn for the worse, however. A message arrived from the King at the beginning of November, citing the Cardinal to a meeting in Mojados, some 75 kilometers from Aranda. This was to be Cisneros' final act as regent: "Once public concerns and specific problems had been discussed and [Cisneros'] suggestions for the organization of the service at court had been received, he could retire to his house and rest. He may then trust that he would receive from God the reward for the labours he had undertaken on behalf of the realm, since no mortal could give him the thanks he deserved. As long as he lived, the King would remember him and have for him the same esteem and consideration as an obedient son toward his good parents." Gómez noted that two versions concerning the King's message were circulating in his time. According to one, Cisneros read the letter, "felt rejected and repulsed, and had a fatal attack of fever." According to the other, Cisneros was already gravely ill the evening before the message arrived, and the letter "was not given to the Cardinal but sent on to the Royal Council" (*De rebus gestis*, 523). The first variant, that a tersely worded letter citing him to Mojados hastened Cisneros' death, is no doubt romantic embroidery. We have Ruiz' letter to Ayala confirming that the instructions to go to Mojados never reached Cisneros. "The Cardinal of Tortosa [Adrian] today sent to the Cardinal the letters that came for the Council concerning the matter of the departure. And in my opinion it was not advisable to give them to him, for it could be that in view of the unfortunate condition of the Cardinal His Highness [King Charles] might change his proposal concerning the journey to Mojados." In a postscript he noted that the Cardinal's health was failing rapidly and had entered a critical phase. The following day, 8 November, Cisneros died, comforted by the sacraments.

According to custom, his body was dressed in clerical robes and laid out, so that the people might file past and kiss his hand. As usual, an indulgence was granted on the occasion. His body was then embalmed and transported to Alcalá, where he was buried. A monument of white marble was erected in his honour, bearing an inscription composed by the humanist Juan Vergara:

> I, Franciscus, founded a great school for the Muses; I myself am laid to rest in a narrow coffin. I combined the purple with sackcloth, the bishop's hat with the helmet. I was a monk and a general, a bishop and a cardinal. My valour united the monk's hood with the crown, when Spain obeyed me as its regent. (Gómez, *De rebus gestis*, 527)

Gómez concludes his account of Cisneros' life with a eulogy of his character and habits:

> He expressed his views with brevity, his replies were pertinent and without digressions; indeed he was very sparing with words, even when he was angry. When he promised to return a favour received, he gave more than he had promised. He rarely spoke about matters that were insignificant. He frequently quoted the saying of Cicero: "Nature has created us, not that we give ourselves over to diversions and pastimes, but that we might

engage in serious matters and worthy enterprises." (*De rebus gestis*, 530)

According to Gómez, the Cardinal was subject to bouts of depression, and on those occasions sought solitude. Otherwise, he had a strong will and much determination, quoting Sallust's "If you have made a decision, carry it out at once." He was devoted to scholarship and "during dinner was in the habit of having questions put to him on certain subjects, especially sacred subjects, and listen to the disputations of learned men who were always present at his table. He often attended the dialectical disputations of young students, for as he said, the good farmer makes use of short sprouts as much as of branches laden with fruit" (*De rebus gestis*, 531). Although generally an austere man, he took great pleasure in a jester, Francesillo by name, whose wit he appreciated. As was the custom of the time, he kept for his amusement a dwarf, Sanchez Pumilion, and a simpleton who entertained him with confused recitations of passages from the Bible.

Gómez provides this detailed description of the Cardinal's appearance:

> He was tall, vigorous, and well proportioned. He walked with a quiet, natural dignity. His voice was strong and even like that of the heroes celebrated by the poet. His face was long and lean, his forehead wide and smooth. His eyes small, sunk rather than protruding, but penetrating and lively and moist like those of people who cry often. His nose was large and curved — like the beak of an eagle, as the Greeks say. The holes of his nose were big and wide. His teeth narrowly spaced, but with the canine teeth protruding so that jokers called him "The Elephant". His lips were quite thick and somewhat open, his upper lip being raised a little, but not excessively. His ears were small, not drooping, but attached along the whole line to the end of the jaw. His upper body was a third larger than his lower body. (*De rebus gestis*, 529–30)

The archbishopric of Toledo, vacated by Cisneros' death, was conferred on Chièvres' nephew. The appointment caused much resentment. The recipient was a teenager and — perhaps an even greater affront to Spanish sensibilities — a foreigner. "There was some muttering in the country," Mexía reports, "when they said that so great a dignity was conferred on a foreigner ... but in these as in other matters the fault was not the King's but of those who, instead of giving him advice concerning the appointment, requested it for themselves" (*Crónica*, 83–4). Martire similarly noted that the appointment was "against the laws and customs of the kingdom" and expressed the fear, moreover, that it "opened the door through which untold quantities of money could leave the country" (Ep. 602, pp. 286–7).

8   *The Image of the Cardinal*

Gómez de Castro gives this account of the Cardinal's reputation in his time:

> Many people thought that Cisneros had a mania for building; others that he had more of a mania for warfare than was proper for a bishop. Many thought that he was a champion of letters and patron of scholars on a grand scale ... The diversity of verdicts stemmed from no other cause but from the fact that once he entered on a task, he devoted all his energies to it, so that it seemed as if he was born for it and a natural disposition had driven him to this undertaking. (*De rebus gestis*, 365)

Gómez put his finger on a trait that was a predominant and striking aspect of the Cardinal's character. He was compulsive in all his actions. Once he had decided on a course of action, he was fanatical in its pursuit. Fanaticism governed his reforms and his missionary activities; singlemindedness characterized his political actions; uncompromising self-discipline his private life. An inability to delegate may have been his weak point. For the sake of keeping charge of affairs, he surrounded himself with mediocre men, whom he could control, who were his devoted servants but never rose to be his disciples or carry on his life's work.

In the seventeenth century the image of the Cardinal became polarized. Some saw in him a saint; others a shrewd politician. Two groups of sources are of particular interest in this context: tracts from the 1650s and '60s supporting the canonization of Cisneros; and a clutch of biographies comparing him with Cardinal Richelieu.

Among the first is Pedro de Quintanilla y Mendoza's *Archetypo de Virtudes, Espexo de Prelados: El Venerable Padre y Siervo de Dios F. Francisco Ximenes de Cisneros* (Archetype of Virtues and Mirror of Prelates: The Venerable Father and Servant of God, Fray Francisco

Ximenes de Cisneros; Palermo, 1653). This eulogy is prefaced by a
letter to Pope Innocent X, dated at the College of San Ildefonso,
1650, and asking for the beatification of the founder. A first application had been prepared in 1633 but went no further. Another attempt in 1650 received the support of the University of Alcalá, but
the efforts of Cisneros' admirers remained without issue and were
abandoned in the eighteenth century. The evidence collected did not
fulfil its designated purpose but it assured Cisneros a saintly reputation. Quintanilla had read widely on his subject in prepration for the
task at hand. He drew on archival material in the University of
Alcalá and on the accounts of the royal historians as well as on
Gómez de Castro's Life. It is evident that he approached his sources
with certain historiographical and research skills. Indeed he made
some factual corrections to the material, but he cannot be called an
objective observer. His purpose and his official commission was to
portray Cisneros as a saint. As can be expected, he minimized nega-
tive aspects, focused on Cisneros' religious reforms and missionary
activities, and capitalized on his "miracles". According to Quintanilla
(and earlier biographers) Cisneros fed his companions with bread
from heaven in the wilderness and produced a sparkling stream of
water to quench their thirst; on another journey he and his companions miraculously survived a shipwreck; a cross appeared in the sky
when he conquered Oran; he "had the wind in his sleeves" when
crossing between Spain and North Africa; heavenly crows pecked out
the eyes of his Moorish enemies; he extinguished a blaze by praying;
he levitated and prayed with such fervor that a "supernatural sweat"
appeared on his brow.

An undated *Responsio ad animadversiones Reverendissimi D. Pro-
mothoris Fidei super dubio an constet de virtutibus theologalibus …*
(Response to the queries of the Most Reverend Promoter of Faith
about doubts regarding [Cisneros'] theological virtues …) provides
information supplementary to the application for beatification and
canonization. It answers questions raised by the authorities concerning the number and character of witnesses cited and addresses concerns about the hearsay nature and dubious historical value of some
of the testimony given. Bound with this volume are *Decreta sacra
rituum congregationis in favorem causae beatificationis et canonizationis
… Francisci Ximenez de Cisneros … a sanctissimis pontificibus …
concessa* (Sacred Decrees of the Congregation of Rites in favour of the

application for the beatification and canonization of Franciscus Ximenez de Cisneros and issued by the most sacred popes; last item dated 1671), which cites briefs from Popes Urban VII, Innocent X, Alexander VII, and Clement IX and X, that is, character references from the highest authorities dating from the sixteenth to the eighteenth century. Another biographical account, *Vida y motivos de la comun aclamación de ... Cisneros* (Madrid, 1673), compiled by Pedro Fernandez de Pulgar, canon of Palencia, was dedicated to the Archbishop of Toledo, Pasqual Cardinal of Aragon. Designed to supply information to the archbishop, "for it is Your Eminence who must receive the communication from the Holy See in order to establish a public cult for the Venerable Servant of God [Cisneros]," it was kept brief "to relieve Your Eminence from reading the rather lengthy documentation." In spite of a promise "to tell some new things unpublished until now," Fernandez de Pulgar presents a well rehearsed story. He does, however, add to the list of miracles, which now includes the fact that Cisneros had control over natural phenomena ("the sun stopped, the winds dropped, the clouds moved, birds descended — the Servant of God ruled them by divine dispensation," p. 28). Another notable feature of this Life is an appendix of "authors which in published works ... have celebrated the virtues, miracles, or deeds of ... Ximenez de Cisneros" — a list containing some 450 entries and spanning two centuries.

Perhaps the most interesting and certainly the most extraordinary testimony to the Cardinal's enduring fame as a saintly man is an anonymous play published in Madrid, 1740. It is ascribed to "a talent at this court" and bears the florid title *Pluma, Purpura, y Espada solo en Cisneros se halla* (Pen, Purple, and Sword are only united in Cisneros). Although the Cardinal's conquest of Oran is the main subject of the play, there is a parallel romantic plot, which justifies its designation as a "new comedy". The action is further lightened by the words and deeds of one "Fray Giropa" (modelled on Francisco Ruiz), who plays Sancho Panza to Cisneros' Don Quijote-like character. The actions and thoughts ascribed to Cisneros are largely historical; the peripheral anecdotes, especially the miracles, closely follow Quintanilla's *Archetypo*. The dramatizations skilfully evoke the Cardinal's character, as described by his early biographers. One scene elaborates on his reluctance to become Isabel's confessor and, later, to accept the arbishopric of Toledo.

Giropa: Is it possible that you can be ungrateful for the zeal shown on your behalf by the Queen in making you archbishop of Toledo, and that you should flee from her?

Cisneros: I am unworthy of such a position.

Giropa: Are you not confessor of Her Highness?

Cisneros: Out of obedience.

Giropa: Well, then, you know what I think, Father? Don't you know that the archbishopric is worth three hundred thousand ducats or more?

Cisneros: And of what importance is that, brother?

Giropa: Of what importance? If they gave me two hundred, I'd accept the mitre, and if it were of Morocco!

Reflecting on Cisneros' reputation at court, Girope cites Martire's description, also quoted by Quintanilla: "You are a second Ambrose of Milan." To convince Cisneros to accept the archbishopric, he launches into a rehearsal of his accomplishments, supplying the audience with the necessary biographical background information. Giropa's eulogy is in effect a summary of the first two chapters of Quintanilla's book and closely adheres to some of the formulations found there.

Cisneros' strict observance of the Franciscan rule offers another occasion for comic relief. In accordance with the rules, he rejects a carriage ride and, to the consternation of his tired companion, insists on walking. He prefers solitude to the temptations of the world, explaining:

Cisneros: In the desert one may enjoy more readily the presence of God.

Giropa: True. But even more so, if one doesn't have to walk on foot.

Cisneros: How, then, would you like to be conveyed?

Giropa: In a carriage ...

Cisneros: This is a rare form of madness. You would like a carriage?

Giropa: I would take even a hired donkey.

Cisneros insists on walking, however. Crossing the wilderness with his companion, he works several miracles. Here the playwright is partly following Quintanilla's account (the miraculous production of bread and water), partly introducing new scenarios (an encounter with robbers). The action of the play eventually moves to Oran which, as Cisneros explains, was captured by human strategy as well as divine dispensation. In this context the narrator tells of the miraculous attack of the birds pecking out the eyes of the Moors, as well as of the appearance of a cross in the sky, and the stalling of the sun to lengthen the day and allow the Spaniards to complete their victory.

The Cardinal's religious fervour provides material for another comic scene. While praying rapturously, he is elevated from the ground.

> Giropa (joining in his prayer): Father, thanks be to God, thanks be to God — but where are you going in this fashion?
>
> Cisneros: What is this you are saying, brother? What are you doing?
>
> Giropa: I'm holding on to your belt to go with you. We're already two and a half yards off the ground.
>
> Cisneros: What are you talking about?
>
> Giropa: It's as I say, Your Excellency. I am telling Your Charity.
>
> Cisneros: Are you dreaming?
>
> Giropa: I would say so, if I weren't so hungry. But when I'm hungry I can't sleep.

Although Cisneros' actions and attitudes supply material for humorous scenes, he himself is not the butt of the humour, but is depicted as a man of honour and principle, frustrated and impeded by smaller minds. The play is more romance than historical drama, and the audience is asked to suspend belief and enter into the imaginary action on stage, but Cisneros remains substantially the historical figure we know: the man of God, the defender of the faith, the patriot, the conquerer of Oran.

No less flattering is the portrait emerging from a group of books in which we find Cisneros' career compared with that of Cardinal Richelieu, chief minister to Louis XIII. The earliest such comparison appeared some fifty years after Richelieu's death in Marsollier's *Histoire de ministère du Cardinal Ximénez* (Toulouse, 1694). In the author's opinion, "there are parallels between their character, their fortune, their policies, their maxims, their enterprises, their successes. Both were magnanimous and had a character that was exalted, proud, impenetrable, and naturally grand. Their emotions complemented their character. They were noble, intrepid, capable of undertaking the most difficult tasks." Both men were patrons on a grand scale: "They both fostered the sciences, the arts, and men of letters. This, no less than their actions, contributed to the reputation they acquired so that even today they are regarded the greatest men that France and Spain has ever brought forth." There were, however, these differences: Cisneros had something in his manner "that occasionally degenerated into rudeness," whereas Richelieu was polite and refined and knew how to accommodate himself to any persons or circumstances. On the other hand, Cisneros was incorruptible, a man of integrity, who loved his people — "a rare, yet necessary quality, in those who want to govern" (avertissement, n. p.)

A decade later, l'abbé Richard published *Parallèle du Cardinal Ximenes, Premier Ministre d'Espagne, et du Cardinal de Richelieu, Premier Ministre de France* (Rotterdam, 1705). He concentrated on the differences between the two statesmen. Religion was the basis for Cisneros' decisions and governed his conduct. This could not be said of Richelieu, who acted purely from political motives. Cisneros lived a chaste life and had no dealings with women, whereas Richelieu was not scrupulous in his conduct. According to Richard, Cisneros was respected, Richelieu feared. "If Richelieu surpassed Cardinal Ximénes in politics, Cardinal Ximénes was more famous for his piety. ... Every day in France one encountered satires aimed at the actions of Cardinal Richelieu, whereas in Spain ... one can read the application made for the canonization of Ximénes. ... Richelieu has always been regarded as a statesman who subordinated religion to politics; Ximénes as a great prelate, who as governor of the Spanish realm, based his decision, not on politics, but on piety and religion" (211–12).

The similarities and discrepancies between the two statesmen remained a fascination with biographers. The subject is discussed in the concluding chapter of the standard nineteenth-century biography by Carl Joseph Hefele, a Catholic theologian at the University of Tübingen. The book, entitled *Der Kardinal Ximenes und die kirchlichen Zustände Spaniens am Ende des 15. und Anfange des 16. Jahrhunderts* (Cardinal Ximenes and the Conditions of the Church in Spain at the end of the fifteenth and beginning of the sixteenth century) was first published in 1851, went through a number of editions, and was translated into French (1856), English (1860), and Spanish (1869,

1879). Hefele focuses his comparison between Cisneros and Richelieu
on three aspects: life, policies, and character. He dramatizes the
events after the two men's return from their respective journeys to
Rome: Richelieu, who had already been elevated to a bishopric, was
welcomed back with honours; Cisneros was "thrown into prison by
his bishop" (*Ximenez*, 536). Both left their diocese, one seeking seclusion, the other success in the world. Hefele notes that Cisneros
advanced steadily in his career, whereas Richelieu suffered temporary
reverses but triumphed over adversity in the end. Both received the
cardinalate in recognition of their services to the crown, but while
Richelieu actively pursued power, Cisneros accepted responsibility
reluctantly. He states that "Cisneros forgave those who wanted to
cast him down and did not avenge personal insults; Richelieu, by
contrast, had his enemies executed and spilled the blood of practically
everyone who opposed him or plotted against him" (ibid., 540). Like
earlier biographers, Hefele is not an unbiased observer, but uses
Richelieu as a dark foil, against which Cisneros' qualities shine more
brightly. He perpetuates the melodramatic story of Charles' letter
reaching Cisneros' house on the eve of his death. He observes that
neither minister was cherished by his sovereign, that both were kept
for their usefulness, but "Louis showed outward respect and consideration for his minister and visited him repeatedly when he fell ill, so
that Richelieu almost literally died in the arms of his sovereign,
whereas Charles avoided meeting Cisneros after landing in Spain, and
insulted this meritorious man on his deathbed, even signing his
dismissal" (ibid., 541). In keeping with the saintly portrait of Cisneros is the assertion that "Richelieu was always looking for an advantage in the misfortunes of his neighbours — Cisneros knew
nothing of such arts" (ibid., 546). More perceptive is Hefele's obser-
vation that both cardinals combined genius with industry. Hefele
furthermore agreed with Marsollier that both Cisneros and Richelieu
showed an unshakeable will in the execution of their plans. He is
also correct in pointing out that Cisneros served capable and energetic rulers, whereas Richelieu's king was weak and left him correspondingly more room for maneuvering. In their religious observances,
finally, they adopted different standards: Richelieu acted like a "respectable man of the world, Cisneros like a saintly ascete" (ibid., 549).

Although the comparisons with Richelieu are ahistorical and, in
the case of Marsollier and Richard, exercises in rhetoric rather than

historiography, they are indicative of a general perception. They reflect the heroic image of Cardinal Cisneros, which was already well established at the turn of the seventeenth century. They continue to train the spotlight on Cisneros' moral qualities, but also represent a slight shift in emphasis from the image of a saintly man to that of a man loyal to God and King.

Turning to the twentieth century, I have already mentioned in my preface the dearth of modern English literature on Cisneros. In Spanish literature, by contrast, the cardinal has always attracted and continues to receive a great deal of scholarly attention. Numerous books and articles have appeared in the last twenty years, culminating in José García Oro's painstakingly researched biography *El Cardenal Cisneros: vida y empresos* (Madrid, 1992/93). In many of these works the Cardinal retains a saintly aura. It is telling that García Oro accepts the account of Alvar Gómez de Castro with complacency. Gómez has painted a masterly portrait, he says. "One may study some facet more closely, clarify some points or obscure circumstances ... but one always has the impression that the outline of his personality remains basically as depicted by Gómez de Castro in his richly coloured pages" (*Cisneros* I: 493). To the present day, then, the Cardinal is accorded by his biographers an unusual measure of consideration. They appear to be reluctant to explore the darker recesses of his life or, if they do, fail to include his flaws in a general reckoning. The lone exception is L. P. Harvey (*Islamic Spain, 1250-1500* [Chicago, 1990]), whose account of Cisneros' attitude to Muslims bristles with indignation, and who calls the brutal treatment they received at his hands "utterly indefensible" (331).

On balance, the Cardinal appears strong-minded, principled, energetic and, like his famous contemporary Thomas More, a "man for all seasons". Stepping from the threshold of the Middle Ages, Cisneros cannot be called a trailblazer; he did, however, march in the vanguard of the political and cultural forces shaping the Renaissance. His promotion from *homo novus* to the position of trusted advisor of monarchs was characteristic of a trend in the political organization of early modern Europe. Renaissance rulers typically consolidated their sovereign power by passing over the landed aristocracy in favour of individuals who were tied to them by personal loyalty and would act as their instruments of power. Cisneros clearly believed in the virtue of a centralized government, and as regent used a pragmatic mixture of dictatorial moves and strategic retreats to maintain the prerogative of the crown wherever possible. This included a religious policy promoting national interests and based on the ideal of "one faith, one king". Thus Cisneros played a supportive role in the efforts of the Spanish monarchs to transform their realm from a feudal into a sovereign territorial state — a development that carried the day in the Renaissance.

As a patron of learning, he recognized the importance of the newly developed art of printing and promoted textual criticism, which underpins the transformation from manuscript to print culture. The University of Alcalá continued the scholastic curriculum (as did all new foundations in the sixteenth century), but also included studies in the three biblical languages. It was one of the earliest institutions to incorporate them into the regular curriculum. Antonio Alvar Ezquerra, author of the most recent study of Cisneros' foundation, offers this enthusiastic assessment:

> "Instruction at the new University of Alcalá de Henares differed in many points from that given at Salamanca, its principal rival. The reason is this: It did not routinely adopt the University of Paris as its model ... Cisneros, with absolute conviction, had, from the inception of the University, planned a new and accurate edition of the Bible based on the premises of humanistic philology, although it was a humanism closer to the spirit of Erasmus than to the paganizing Italians. Consequently, the study of theology at Alcalá, enriched by the *studia humanitatis*, was free of scholastic dogmatism and enlivened by the spirit of tolerance [!] ... Perhaps there was no great substantive difference between the instruction offered at Salamanca and Alcalá, but there was in spirit. It is significant in this sense that the Cisnerian university contacted Erasmus and Vives, inviting them to come and teach there. In effect, the university preferred the method of rhetorical exegesis, a humanistic heritage, to the method of dogmatic exposition in the scholastic tradition. ("Le modèle," 245–6)

As a church leader Cisneros likewise foreshadowed developments that were soon to dominate Europe: the call for spiritual renewal and for a new approach to theology, focusing on biblical studies. Anticipating a movement that gathered momentum during the Counter-

Reformation, he called for pastoral responsibility, for a sober life reflecting the vows of chastity and poverty, and for the study of biblical texts in their original languages. His support for the Beatas, which strikes the modern reader as bordering on superstition, should be regarded in the context of the pious yearning which characterized pre-Reformation Europe. It found expression in the mysticism of German *Schwärmer* and Italian *spirituali*. Spain, more than any other country, provided a fertile ground for religious enthusiasm. Although some of the Spanish *alumbrados* and *dejados* were accused of heterodoxy because they appeared to challenge the hierarchy of the church, mysticism also attracted distinguished Catholic reformers like Loyola and Teresa of Avila. Rooted in medieval sensitivities, mystics remained a feature of the religious landscape in the Counter-Reformation. Both in his mystical leanings and in the intolerance Cisneros showed toward non-Christians, he manifested the cultural bias of his time. His "crusade" in North Africa and his inquisitorial proceedings in Granada leave modern readers with a feeling of distaste. His militant spirit especially, and his desire to lay down his life for God and win a martyr's crown, which was heroic in the eyes of his early biographers, appears today as a facet of cultural and religious imperialism.

In spite of such flaws, Cisneros was remarkable for his versatility. In his recent biography, Cruz Martínez Esteruelas describes Cisneros as excelling in the three principal aspects of human nature: he was a *homo religiosus, homo politicus*, and *homo oeconomicus*, that is, a spiritual, political, and practical man (*Cisneros*, 178–9). It cannot be denied that Cisneros played a pivotal role in Spanish history. If there is a perception today that he does not belong to the select circle of those who changed the course of history, it is because his political ideas, his zeal for reform, and his interest in print culture and philology, progressive at the time, became mainstream within a decade of his death. Thus time caught up with Cisneros. His thought merged with the *Zeitgeist* and became invisible in the broad currents of the Renaissance.

Literature Cited

Abbreviations

ACA	Archivo de la Corona de Aragón (Barcelona) (now titled in Catalan Arxiu de la Corona de Aragó)
AHN	Archivo Histórico Nacional (Madrid)
AIA	*Archivo Ibero Americano*
Allen	P. S. Allen, ed., *Erasmi Epistolae*, 12 vols. (Oxford, 1906–58)
Alvar Esquerra	A. Alvar Esquerra, "Alvar Gómez de Castro y la historiografia latina," in *El Erasmismo en España*, ed. M. Revuelta Sañudo et al. (Santander, 1986), 247–64
Alvar Esquerra, "Le modèle"	"Le modèle universitaire d'Alcalá de Henares dans la première moitié du XVIe siècle," in *Les origines du Collège de France (1500–1560)*, ed. M. Fumaroli (Paris, 1998), 209–57
Andres	M. Andres, *La teología española en el siglo XVI*, vol. 2 (Madrid, 1977)
Bataillon	M. Bataillon, *Erasmo y España* (Mexico, 1966)
Bentley	J. Bentley, *Humanists and Holy Writ* (Princeton 1983)
Bergenroth	G. A. Bergenroth, ed., *Calendar of Letters and Papers ... England and Spain* (London, 1862)
CMH	*The New Cambridge Modern History*, ed. D. Hay (first ed., Cambridge, 1957), vol. 1
Cart. Sec.	*Cartas de los secretarios del Cardenal ... Ximénez de Cisneros durante su regencia ...*, ed. V. de la Fuente (Madrid, 1875)

Cart. Xim. *Cartas del Cardenal ... Ximénez de Cisneros ...*, ed. P. Gayangos y V. de la Fuente (Madrid, 1867)

Cedillo Conde de Cedillo, *El Cardenal Cisneros, gobernador del Reino*, 3 vols. (Madrid, 1921–28)

Constituciones R. Gonzáles Navarro, ed. and trans., *Universidad Complutense. Constituciones originales cisnerianas* (Alcalá, 1984)

CWE *The Collected Works of Erasmus* (Toronto, 1974–)

Davies R. Trevor Davies, *The Golden Century of Spain: 1501–1621* (London, 1937)

Díaz-Plaja F. Díaz-Plaja, ed., *Historia de España en sus documentos* (Madrid, 1988)

Elliott, *Spain* J. H. Elliott, *Imperial Spain 1469–1716* (New York, 1963)

Elliott, *World* J. H. Elliott, *The Hispanic World: Civilisation and Empire* (London, 1991)

Escandell Bonet B. Escandell Bonet, *Estudios Cisnerianos* (Alcalá, 1990)

García Oro, *Cisneros* J. García Oro, *El Cardenal Cisneros: Vida y empresas*, 2 vols. (Madrid, 1992–3)

García Oro, *Reforma* J. García Oro, *Cisneros y la reforma del clero español en tiempo de los Reyes Católicos* (Madrid, 1971)

Gilly C. Gilly, "Una obra desconocida de Nebrija contra Erasmo y Reuchlin," in *El Erasmismo en España*, ed. M. Revuelta Sañudo et al. (Santander, 1986), 195–218

Gómez, *De rebus gestis* A. Gómez, *De rebus gestis a Francisco Ximeni Cisnerio*, Spanish trans. J. Oroz Reta (Madrid, 1984)

Hefele, *Ximenez* C. von Hefele, *The Life and Times of Cardinal Ximenez*, trans. J. C. Dalton (2nd ed., London, 1885)

Harvey L. P. Harvey, *Islamic Spain: 1250–1500* (Chicago, 1990)

Hamilton   A. Hamilton, *Heresy and Mysticism in Sixteenth-Century Spain: The alumbrados* (Toronto, 1992)

Hillgarth   J. Hillgarth, *The Spanish Kingdoms 1250–1516* (Oxford, 1978) vol. 2

Historical   *Historical Catalogue of the Printed Editions of Holy*
Catalogue   *Scripture in the Library of the British and Foreign Bible Society*, eds. T. Darlow and H. Moule (New York, 1963) vol. 2, # 1517

History of   B. de las Casas, *History of the Indies*, trans. A. Col-
the Indies   lard (New York, 1971)

Kamen, *Spain*   H. Kamen, *Spain 1469–1714: A Society in Conflict* (London, 1983)

Kamen,   H. Kamen, *Inquisition and Society in Spain* (Bloom-
Inquisition   ington, 1985)

Ladero Quesada   M. Ladero Quesada, *Los mudéjares de Castilla en tiempo de Isabel* (Valladolid, 1969)

Liss   P. Liss, *Isabel the Queen: Life and Times* (New York, 1992)

Mariéjol   J. H. Mariéjol, *The Spain of Ferdinand and Isabella*, trans. B. Keen (New Brunswick, 1961)

Marineo Siculo   L. Marineo Siculo, *Epistolarum Familiarium libri* (Valladolid, 1514)

Martínez Esteruelas   C. Martínez Esteruelas, *Cisneros, de presidiario a rey* (Barcelona, 1992)

Martire   P. Martire, *Opus epistolarum* (Alcala, 1530); Spanish version by J. López de Toro in *Documentos inéditos para la historia de España* (Madrid 1953–57), vols. 9–12. In the text I quote by the number of the letter ("Ep").

Menéndez Pidal   R. Menéndez Pidal, "The Significance of the Reign of Isabella the Catholic According to Her Contemporaries," in *Spain in the Fifteenth Century*, ed. R. Highfield (London, 1972), 380–404

Merriman   R. B. Merriman, *The Rise of the Spanish Empire* (New York, 1962), vol. 2

Meseguer   J. Meseguer Fernández, "Documentos históricos diversos. III: El Cardenal Cisneros inquisidor general," *AIA*: 43 (1983): 95–194

Mexía, *Crónica*   Pero Mexía in *Collección de Crónicas Españolas*, ed. J. de Mata Carriazo, vol. 7 (Madrid, 1945)

Moorman   J. Moorman, *The History of the Franciscan Order* (Oxford, 1968)

Nebrija,   A. Nebrija, *Apologia cum quibusdam Sacrae Scrip-*
Apologia   *turae locis non vulgariter expositis* (n.l., 1516)

Novum   D. Erasmus, ed., *Novum Instrumentum* (Basel, 1516);
Instrumentum   called *Novum Testamentum* in later editions

Olin   J. Olin, *Catholic Reformation From Cardinal Ximenes to the Council of Trent, 1495–1563* (New York, 1990)

Pérez   J. Pérez, ed., *La hora de Cisneros* (Madrid, 1995)

Prescott   Wm. Prescott, *History of the Reign of Ferdinand and Isabella*, (first published 1883; 10th ed., New York, 1951)

Quintano   Quintano Ripollés, *Historia de Alcalá de Henares* (Alcalá, 1973)

Quintanilla   P. Quintanilla, *Archetypo de virtudes. Espejo de prelados* (Palermo, 1653)

RABM   A. de la Torre, "La Universidad de Alcalá. Datos para su historia," *Revista de Archivos, Bibliotecas y Museos* 21 (1909): 48–71, 261–85, 405–33

Retana,   L. Fernández de Retana, *Cisneros y su siglo*, 2 vols.
Cisneros   (Madrid, 1929)

Rodríguez Sánchez   A. Rodríguez Sánchez, *Historia de España* (Madrid, 1991)

Sainz Rodríguez   P. Sainz Rodríguez, *La siembra mística del Cardenal Cisneros y las reformas en la iglesia* (Madrid, 1979)

Rummel   E. Rummel, *The Humanist-Scholastic Debate in the Renaissance and Reformation* (Cambridge, Mass., 1995)

Telechea   J.-I. Telechea, "La reforma religiosa," in Pérez, *La Hora de Cisneros*, 43–53

Tibesar   A. S. Tibesar, "The Franciscan Province of the Holy Cross of Española," *The Americas* 13 (1957): 377–89

Vallejo   J. de Vallejo, *Memorial de la vida de Fray Francisco Jimenez de Cisneros*, ed. A. de la Torre y del Cerro (Madrid, 1913)

Wadding   L. Wadding, *Annales Minorum ab origine Ordinis ad annum 1540*, 25 vols. (Rome, 1731–1886)

Witness   *Witness: Writings of Bartolomé de las Casas*, ed. G. Sanderlin, foreword by D. Gutierrez (New York, 1992)

Further Reading

Di Camillo, O.   "Humanism in Spain," in *Renaissance Humanism: Foundations, Forms, and Legacy*, ed. A. Rabil (Philadelphia, 1988), 2: 55–108

Farge, J. K.   *Le Parti conservateur au XVIe siècle: Université et Parlement de Paris à l'époque de la Renaissance et de la Réforme* (Paris, 1992), VII: "Les lecteurs royaux et la Bible"

Fernández-Armesto, F.   "Jiménez de Cisneros," in *Contemporaries of Erasmus. A Biographical Register of the Renaissance and Reformation*, ed. P. Bietenholz and T. Deutscher (Toronto, 1986), 2: 235–7

Hall, B.   *Humanists and Protestants, 1500–1900* (Edinburgh, 1990), chapter 1: "Cardinal Jiménez de Cisneros and the Complutensian Polyglot" (based on the Birkbeck Lectures in Ecclesiastical History, 1975)

Lyell, J. P. R.   *Cardinal Ximenes, Statesman, Ecclesiastic, Soldier and Man of Letters* (London, 1917)

Maltby, W.   "Jiménez de Cisneros," in *The Oxford Encyclopedia of the Reformation*, ed. J. Hillerbrand (Oxford, 1996), 2: 345–46

Merton, R.   *Cardinal Ximenes and the Making of Spain* (London, 1934)

Starkie, W.   *Grand Inquisitor: Being an Account of Cardinal Ximenez de Cisneros and His Times* (London, 1940)

Appendix 1: The Constitution of San Ildefonso College

The conduct of college residents was regulated by a constitution, drawn up in 1510. The following chapters, translated from the edition of Ramon Gonzáles Navarro, *Universidad Complutense, Constitutiones originales cisnerianas* (Alcalá, 1984), 180–347, give a picture of life in the college and the regulations governing it. A concise descriptive account can be found in Antonio Alvar Ezquerra's "Le modèle universitaire d'Alcalá de Henares dans la première moitié du XVIe siècle," in *Les origines du Collège de France (1500–1560)*, ed. M. Fumaroli (Paris, 1998), 209–56.

The head of the college was the rector, who was elected annually by and from among the members of the college (*collegiales*). He was aided in his decisions by three councillors elected in the same fashion. The college also had twelve chaplains, whose duties included the administration of the college and who remained in office four years. Apart from the thirty-three regular members of the college, there were also *porcionistas*, laymen who paid for their board, and *cameristas*, who participated in the government of the college in their special area of expertise. A dozen servants, responsible for the household tasks, also lived in the college.

Chapter 1: The Members of the College

First of all, it has been our decision that in the College which we [Cisneros] have had constructed from the foundations within the walls of our city of Alcalá de Henares, with divine aid and under the name and protection of Saint Ildefonso, there will be thirty-three prebendaries [holders of stipendiary positions] in perpetuity. One of them will be the Head and Rector of the whole College and University. Apart from the aforesaid prebendaries, there will be in the same College twelve secular priests serving as chaplains ... In addition there will be in the same College twelve *familiares* [housekeeping personnel]. One of them will be in charge of provisions, another will be the cook; the remaining ten will assume general household tasks.

Chapter 2: The Rector and Councillors of the College

We ordain that each year on the eve of St Luke the Evangelist a Rector and three Councillors be elected from among the thirty-three prebendaries, whose task it will be to govern the College and keep order in it. In this election, the chaplains have the right neither to vote nor to stand for election, for we do not wish them to be included under the term *collegiales* [Fellows].

Chapter 6: Vacant Prebends and the Election of Fellows

If a prebend in our College falls vacant, the Rector must announce the vacancy within three days in the dining hall, after dinner. Failure to do so will result in his being penalized by the loss of his dinner portions for one month. He may pay the College for his portion to avoid being absent from dinner. Once the vacancy has been announced, none of the Fellows is allowed to leave the College until the vacancy is filled. Failure to comply will result in the loss of one outfit or the equivalent value in cash. An exception can be made in an urgent case, with the permission of the Rector, but the vote cannot be assigned to a proxy. On the day of the announcement the Rector must call and conduct a closed meeting to decide whether it is expedient or not to send notices to other universities. If it is thought to be expedient ... let the notices be affixed to the doors of the universities, so that those who wish to enter the competition may come and do so ... [Next, the Rector and Fellows will] diligently inquire into the character and qualifications of the candidates and examine them ... [Fifteen days later] a mass of the Holy Spirit is celebrated. The Rector calls a closed meeting, asks each and everyone of the Fellows present for an oath that he will in the presence of God, without any bias, inclination, or favour, elect the man who is best qualified and most suitable, principally taking into consideration his academic qualifications, his integrity, and his cooperation; and the Rector similarly swears an oath to this effect. This done, a sheet of paper is given to each and every one of the Fellows, on which the full names of the candidates are written ... [candidates are forbidden to influence the Fellows; similarly the Fellows are forbidden to] reveal their choice through words, signs, gestures, or letters. [The election itself follows the same pattern as the election of the Rector; the complex procedure is described in detail in chapter 3].

Chapter 7: The Qualifications of Fellows and the Duration of Fellowships

The minimum age [for Fellows] is twenty, and the candidate must have completed the *Summulae* [basic course in logic], so that he may be competent in logic. He must be poor, that is, at the time of election his income from benefices or an inheritance must not exceed twenty-five Aragonese gold florins. ... His major should not be in canon law or medicine ... for we have founded the College primarily for the benefit of studies in the Arts and in Sacred Theology ... We do not wish them to be natives of the town of Alcalá, ... for they can attend lectures and disputations without having prebends in the College. Nor do we wish that two or three closely related persons be elected Fellows ... nor anyone who is engaged to a woman or has entered a religious order ... Those who have been elected have the right to hold the fellowship continuously for eight years. For the duration of their stay in College each Fellow and chaplain will receive a room with his own key, food, clothing as detailed below, medicine and the services of a physician, candles (one each night, ten of them weighing a pound), the services of a barber and laundress; a wooden bed, equipped; also a table, chair, and bench ... It is forbidden to keep kindling in the bedrooms or anywhere else in the College, to prevent any risk of fire and other inconveniences.

Chapter 8: Dress and Deportment

[Once a year members of the College were issued a hooded cloak, which was to be worn whenever they went outside the College precincts.] No one is to go outside the College dressed otherwise or without being accompanied by one of his colleagues or without the express permission of the rector ... we further wish that none of the aforesaid persons grow a beard or long hair; rather they should resemble respectable secular priests in their appearance. None of them is permitted to go into town to have lunch or dinner there, unless by permission of the rector, which should not be easily obtained ... Let no one presume to bear arms either openly or concealed, or have arms in their own rooms on penalty of being deprived of their portion for a month and having the weapon confiscated. Let them beware of all seditious talk or scandal, especially in the dining hall. Anyone in violation of this shall be punished harshly by the rector, depending on the social status of the person and other circumstances.

No one is allowed to play dice or cards, and we strictly forbid any kind of musical instrument in our College, with the exception of monochord or cembalo (*monochordium, clavicimbalum*). Let them not spend too much time on music or impose on others. On feast days, and with the express permission of the rector, regents and members of the College are permitted to take part in games among themselves or with students, such as the game of *pile, saxi, ferri*, and other such physical exercises, with the proviso that they do not interfere with lectures and other exercises, should these be scheduled for those days; provided also that they play these games in the interior part of the building or patio or other place where they cannot be observed from the outside. And let the rector not grant such permission lightly, but only when he sees that the work must be lightened with these kinds of respectable pastimes. If anyone presumes to do these things contrary to our constitution, he shall be deprived, on the first offense, of his portion for a day, on the second offense, of his portion for a week, on the third, of his portion for a month. ...

We furthermore forbid that any women be given access to the College at any time, except by permission of the rector, who must not grant such permission without consideration for the social status and dignity of the person and the justice of the cause. And in that case, let him appoint a person of integrity to be her guide and show her the buildings of the College.

Chapter 10: Absence from the College
If any of the prebendaries or chaplains wish to absent themselves, they may take two months after personally seeking the permission of the rector. He must give permission, unless there is just cause for believing that the permission should be denied or delayed. For this reason we wish that any chaplain or prebendary seek the said permission at least one day before his departure. If, however, there is an urgent need for his departure and delaying it by one day would mean some risk, the rector must give him the required permission immediately, after the applicant has confirmed the said urgency by an oath. No chaplain or prebendary is allowed to leave the College before giv-

ing surety for his debts and fulfilling any obligations to the College. Nor is he permitted to be absent for more than two months, except when there is an urgent reason, [in which case he may be allowed to be absent for another term of two months]. ... When this second term has elapsed and the absent chaplain or member of the College has not returned, he loses his prebend or chaplaincy. ... If anyone has lost his prebend or chaplaincy on account of absence or another reason, he may not stand for a competition again, because we do not wish that a person who has once been deprived of his prebend or chaplaincy be admitted to it again. However, if someone was detained by a grave illness or undeserved incarceration he will not lose his residence. He must show an authentic, notarized document to prove that he was detained and cite four witnesses who can testify to it under oath before a judge. One of the witnesses must be a physician, if he was detained by illness. Once the said four months have elapsed, the prebend must not be declared vacant immediately, but there must be a waiting period of fifteen days to give the person in question an opportunity to prove that he was detained by incarceration or illness, as we have said.

Chapter 15: Dining Arrangements

Tablecloths, serviettes or napkins should be changed every week. Every day silver cups ... which we have given to the College, are to be distributed among the rector, the chaplains, and members of the College, so that beverages may be served to the members in a becoming fashion ... Each of them will also be given a knife, a salt shaker, and a jar of water ... and everyone will eat the same quantity of food, prepared in the same manner. The hour of lunch and dinner varies according to the time of the year and will be established by the rector and the councillors, unless a majority disagrees with them. No one is to be served any food outside the dining hall ... We further provide that during lunch and dinner in the dining hall spiritual readings shall not be neglected. Ordinarily the Bible shall be read at lunch; at dinner other books of saints or doctors may be read, as long as they are approved by the church, and according to the judgment of the rector and the councillors. ... Since it may happen that a reader at table pronounces the words in an incongruous or unlearned fashion, the mistakes of the reader should be corrected by a senior regent of theology in attendance, and if the theologians are absent, by a senior regent of arts, or a *baccalarius formatus* in theology, or other masters according to seniority, or someone else to whom the rector has entrusted this task. But let all beware of seditious mumbling and scandal and noise, so that the reader may be heard attentively by all — on threat of a harsh penalty according to the seriousness of the matter and the social status of the person. The penalty is to be set and executed by the rector.

No one who resides in our College is allowed to enter the kitchen or the cellar except those whose business it is to be in the cellars or in the kitchen to prepare or season the food. The said employees must keep their workplace locked on penalty to be determined by the rector. Anyone other than an employee found entering these places ... will be deprived of his portion of wine for the day, or if the rector so decides, of the whole food portion of the day. To allow them to keep warm, we do permit, however, that during the winter a fire be lit shortly before lunch and dinner in some respectable place, and with the rules of modesty being observed. In the dining hall, however, there shall be no open fire.

Chapter 18: Security
We decree, moreover, that all gates of the College be locked in the following order by a servant designated for this task. The main gate pointing north shall always be locked at dusk. The gate pointing south which leads to the patio of the servants shall be locked at different times according to the season: from the feastday of St. Luke to the feast of the Purification of the Virgin at seven p.m.; from the feast of the Purification until Pentecost at eight; from Pentecost until the feast of the Assumption of the Virgin at nine; from the Assumption until the feastday of St. Luke again at eight. Fifteen minutes before the gate is locked the large bell shall be rung and shortly before it is locked the bell shall be rung nine times to warn the visitors, that those living outside the College may leave ... a janitor shall stand by the gate to watch those entering and leaving. If he observes anything detrimental to the reputation of the College, he is bound to report it to the rector immediately. ... When all the gates are shut, the aforesaid janitor shall give the keys to the junior councillor. Non-compliance will be punished with incarceration by sentence of the rector. The said councillor is under obligation to examine the locks of the gates after he has received the keys, on

penalty of losing his portion for a week. If by chance a visitor remains in the building after the gates are shut, he is under no circumstances allowed to spend the night in the College. Nor shall a gate be opened to allow him to leave, but he shall be lowered by a rope from a window. However, should an emergency arise after all gates of the building are shut, for example, the need for a physician or for medication or a similar matter that is too dangerous to neglect or delay — in that case the gate of the servants, that is, the one pointing west or the other gate of the College pointing south may be opened in the presence of the rector and councillors. Anyone who attempts to unlock one of the gates under other circumstances, shall immediately be expelled from the College and never again be admitted.

Chapter 23: The College Library
We decree that the books in the library which we have built in the College and which we have supplied with a sufficient quantity of books, shall at all times be chained by their individual chains in their proper place, so that they may not easily be taken away; and we forbid that they be lent to anyone. That all who want to use the library may have easy access and without difficulty may take advantage of its facilities, we wish that the said library be open throughout the year for four hours every day, in this manner: from the feast day of St. Luke until the Resurrection every day in the morning from eight to ten and in the afternoon from two to four. And from the Resurrection to the feastday of St. Luke, mornings from seven to nine and afternoons from three to five. ... Fellows and chaplains shall have their private keys to the library but shall not be permitted to leave the door to the library unlocked. If anyone has been negligent in this matter, he shall be deprived of his portion for one day each time this happens; if a visitor to the College comes to the library at an hour other than the normal opening hours, the person who unlocks the door for him must wait and watch at the door until the visitor leaves. Anyone ... taking a book from the library will be deprived of his ordinary portion and kept from the table for 15 days on the first infraction; on the second the penalty will be doubled; on the third he shall be expelled from the College. If the person is a visitor, he incurs automatically a sentence of excommunication, from which he can only be absolved by the rector after giving satisfaction. The books in the library must be dusted and cleaned in turn by one

of the junior chaplains or Fellows together with a servant, at least once a month. And one of the servants must clean the floor of the library in their presence. Anyone negligent in this task shall be punished by a penalty to be determined by the Rector. The Rector and the regents [holders of Chairs] as well as the *magistri* in theology are exempted from this labour.

Chapter 35: The Appointment of Professors and Lecturers: The Summulist [teacher of basic logic]
The Rector and councillors of the College and university shall appoint one or two days on which the candidates will lecture, one after the other. And they shall assign them lecture topics from the *Summulae*, topics which the students who have a vote will best understand. Each candidate shall lecture on these texts, including the proper questions and replies in the Parisian manner, as outlined below. If a candidate presents himself who is not a graduate or member of this university, he must give ten lectures within the stipulated period (to avoid delaying the appointment), so that his scholarship and aptitude can be determined. The *magistri* of theology and arts, who are not lecturing at that time, are to be present together with the Rector and the councillors and the students who will have to take the course in *Summulae* that year. When the candidates have given their lectures, the Rector together with the councillors shall call a closed meeting and there admonish the students to give due consideration to their choice of candidates, since they will have to take the course in *Summulae* and everything else required for completion of the M.A. in four years from him exclusively. The Rector should point out these and other such things that will allow them to make a better and more independent choice. Next, he shall take from each of them an oath confirmed by the sign of the cross and the holy Gospels of God, that they will put out of minds all hatred, favour, or inclination and shall have before their eyes only God and the advantage of the College and university and their own progress, and will vote in consideration of this for the better and more capable man, from whom they expect to benefit more as far as scholarship is concerned. They further swear that they expect to attend for the full academic year the lectures of the person appointed to the chair by the Rector and the councillors. Once this oath is taken, the Rector shall give each student sheets with the first and last names of each candidate so that

they may elect whom they prefer and place the paper [with his name] in the place designated for that purpose. The candidates whom they reject must be clearly separated and placed in a place designated for this purpose, so that any occasion for fraud be removed. When the votes have been gathered in this manner, the Rector and councillors swear an oath that they shall not disclose the votes obtained by each of the candidates, count the votes, and appoint to the chair the person whom they find to have the most votes, without regard for his social status or that of the voters. And the new appointee swears an oath [of office] and shall lecture for the following four years. ...

[Two examiners shall be appointed to determine questions of professional conduct] and how many or how few students a lecturer has. They must give to the Rector and councillors a detailed confidential report on the information they have gathered. ... If they decide that one of the professors or of the students significantly compromises the reputation of the College and university through their behaviour or their carelessness, neglect, and incompetence, they will take the necessary steps. If the majority so decides, the professor or lecturer will be deprived of his chair or lectureship without hearing or appeal. ... and if a lecturer is found to have no students or only a few, the Rector may, after due consideration for the time and quality of the lecture, combine it with another one given by the same lecturer or in another faculty, as he thinks best.

Chapter 39: The Examination for the Bachelor of Arts

The student to be examined shall sit before the examiners in a lower seat, bareheaded in the Parisian manner. And the first examiner shall ask a true-or-false question based on the *Summulae*. And when the candidate has given his answer, three examiners will argue against his response by attacking each premise. Next, the first examiner asks the candidate to recite a chapter from the *Liber praedicabilium* of Porphyry ... and the candidate must reply from memory and that examiner alone argues against his reply concerning one premise. Then the second examiner shall ask and argue in the same manner concerning the *Liber predicamentorum*; and the third concerning the *Liber peri hermenias*. Then it is the first examiner's turn again to ask questions about [Aristotle's] *Prior Analytics* and so forth according to the sequence of books and instructors. ... Once the questions concerning logic are finished, they go on to [Aristotle's] *Physics*, although the examination need not be as rigorous as in logic. There shall be only one question or proposition concerning the *Physics* and none concerning *De caelo* or the other books up to the preface of *De anima*. Here the examination ends. That done, the examiners withdraw and discuss whether the candidate's answers were satisfactory and whether he should be awarded the degree. If all or the majority agree that he qualifies, they sign the form which the student has been given by his professor confirming that the requirements have been fulfilled. They then go on to the next candidate, but there shall not be more than two examinations per day. . . . Each bachelor must pay one florin into the common account of the College, one florin to the faculty, two florins to his professor, another florin to be divided equally between the examiners, half a florin for the notary, and half a florin for the beadles, the total sum for the B.A. not to exceed six florins. We furthermore prohibit that the aforesaid examination for the B.A. and any other degree take place in private or in secret. Rather it is to take place publicly in the halls of the College. Otherwise the examination is null and void.

Chapter 58: Extraordinary Chairs
So that everything relevant to the knowledge of letters be available at our College and university, we decree that there should be a chair in Greek, to be held by a regular professor who is sufficiently knowledgable in that language. He is to lecture on regular days within the College for two hours and supervise exercises for one hour. His salary will be fifty florins per year . . . but since men in orders and other persons zealous for the faith and burning with the love of God may wish to learn [other] languages to enable them better to disseminate the word of God, we decree, if there happen to be interested persons in the College, that the Rector and councillors together with a number of faculty called together for this purpose may institute chairs in accordance with their pious and honest wish . . . but if there is a shortage of suitably qualified students, payment will cease. But because Greek is the fountain and origin of the Latin language and of the other sciences, any number of students who could benefit from this language will be considered a sufficient number. If there are none, payment for the chair will cease.

Chapter 62: The Compulsory Use of Latin within the College

We decree that everyone — Rector, professors, chaplains, Fellows, servants, associates, and all others, regardless of whether they are graduates of this university or not, must speak Latin when they are within the College. This includes the chapel, dormitories, dining hall, lecture halls, gardens, library and all other official areas within the precinct of the College. They must speak Latin in their conclusions, disputations, as well as in familiar and daily conversation, in whatever manner and concerning whatever subject they are conversing. If anyone is caught speaking a language other than Latin ... he shall be deprived of his portion of wine at the next meal on the first offense, the whole portion at the next meal on the second offence, and a daily ration on the third offense. If he is found in continuous violation for eight days, he shall have to pay for the value of his clothing for that year. And if he appears to be incorrigible and insists that he does not wish to speak Latin, he shall be expelled from the College ... if those who commit these infractions are under age, they shall be administered the strap or whipped, depending on the frequency of their infraction, for there is no purpose in making rules, unless they are also enforced.

Chapter 66: Respectability

We have decreed moreover that no one in the university may presume to carry arms publicly, inside or outside the College. Those who act to the contrary forfeit the arms ... Furthermore, if anyone in the university is found to have publicly taken a concubine, he shall lose his chair or lectureship or office, if he is a regular professor, lecturer, or official of the College or university; and any other member of the university, whatever his social standing or eminence, shall be expelled. We also prohibit that anyone of the preceding persons have in his house women of ill repute. Anyone who acts to the contrary will be warned in the name of the Rector, and if he does not expel her from his house, will be punished according to the judgment of the Rector. Furthermore, since lack of physical hygiene indicates a corresponding mental quality, it behooves those who labour in the study of letters to give evidence of their profession in their behaviour and external appearance. Therefore we exhort every one in this university to behave respectably and in all other things act with dignity.

Chapter 71: The Reading of the Regulations

To make our constitutions known to all and so that no one may pretend ignorance of the contents, we decree that a copy of these rules be on display in the library of the College, chained in a place where everyone has easy access to it ... and in addition we wish to have these rules read once a year immediately after the feast of St. Luke in the dining hall at lunch and dinner so that it may come to the full attention of each and every person living in the College.

Appendix 2: An Anonymous Life of Cardinal Cisneros

The following translation is based on the Spanish text printed in "An Early Life of Francisco Jiménez de Cisneros," ed. L. Nelson and A. Weiss in *Franciscan Studies* 42 (1982): 156–65. The text is transcribed from a manuscript in the Kenneth Spencer Research Library of the University of Kansas (MS C238), which contains a number of items dated 1524–1541 and relating to the monastery of La Madre de Dios in Cisneros' birthplace, Tordelaguna. A reference on fol. 5r referring to Charles as "emperor" provides a terminus post quem of 1519. The editors suggest that the Life is in the same hand as another document with the date "1524". Thus the present biographical sketch probably dates from the mid-twenties. From internal evidence we know that the author of the Life was, like Cisneros, a Franciscan and may have been present at the opening ceremony of the University of Alcalá. He writes in a sober style and without flattery. In fact, as the modern editors note, "the absence of hyperbole is one of the oustanding characteristics of the work" (p. 159). The text is also remarkable for its precision in establishing the date and location of the events mentioned. In the following translation, I have retained the spelling of proper names as found in the manuscript.

Text
In the name of God. Amen.

This is the history of the founder of this convent and the house of La Madre de Dios in the village of Torrelaguna. He was an outstanding man, called Brother Francisco Ximenez de Çisneros, a native of this place, Torrelaguna, of respectable and honest parents. And in his youth he decided to adopt clerical status in preference to leading a secular life. And in proportion to his maturity, capacity, and learning, Our Lord raised him to diverse positions of honour, one after another, such as we have never seen in any mortal before.

At first, after he had studied law at Salamanca and was already an established scholar, he came to this village of Torrelaguna and was given, in view of his learning and virtues, the archpriesthood of Uzeda. And from this position he rose to become Capellan Mayor of Siguenca and chief judge in spiritual and temporal matters in the whole archbishopric.

And, not content with this state of things, since he thought it was mingled with worldly matters, he decided to go to the city of Toledo. And he was at the monastery of San Juan de los Reyes and there, with much effort and importunity, begged and besought a reverend father by name of Fray Juan de Tolosa, who was provincial of Castile, to allow him to wear the habit of our father St. Francis. And the said provincial, seeing his humility and zeal, gave him permission, acceding to his wishes. And after having been accepted, he made his profession to which he adhered until his death.

After he had taken the habit, he wanted to live a stricter life of rigorous penance and stayed at Nuestra Señora del Castañar, which is six leagues outside of Toledo, and he remained there for some years. And later, they made him Guardian of the same house of Castañar. And while he was there, he led a very strict life of rigorous penance, mortifying his body with prayer, abstinence, and discipline.

And at that time the powerful and Catholic Kings, Don Fernando IV [sic] and his wife Doña Ysabel, daughter of the King Don Juan of illustrious memory, were reigning in our realms of Castile. The Queen determined to make the said Father, who was Guardian of Castañar, her confessor, for her ears had been filled with good report and praise for his life.

And then, at one time, when he was Guardian of La Salzeda, near Tendilla, a provincial chapter was held for the province of Castile in a House and monastery called Sant Istevan, a league outside of Burgos. At this general assembly [Cisneros] was elected Vicar Provincial of Castile in absentia. The outgoing provincial was a religious, who was a scholar and a Professor of Theology, called Maestro Manuel.

At that time Our Lord took from this life the illustrious and noble Señor called Don Pero Goncalez de Mendoza, of illustrious memory, Archbishop of the Church of Toledo and Cardinal of Spain. He died in the city of Gualdaljara on 10 January 1495, and his body was taken to the cathedral of Toledo. And the said Catholic Kings decided, since the said Father [Cisneros] was Provincial, to choose him for the position of Archbishop of the Holy Church of Toledo, for they believed that he had the qualities required for the position. And so he was ordained and invested with the power of the archbishop in Taraçona in the church of the Franciscans on 11 October, a week after the feastday of our Father St. Francis, in the year of the Lord 1495.

And not much later the aforementioned King Fernando, on his return from Italy, brought him the cardinal hat, which put him in charge of all of the Spanish realms, and his title was Cardinal of Santa Balbina. And when he was Archbishop, the Queen of illustrious memory, the Señora Doña Ysabel passed from this life. And her death fell on a Tuesday, the day after St. Catherine's Day, which is the 26 of November in the year of the Lord 1504. It took place at Medina del Campo, and afterwards her body was taken for burial to the city of Granada.

The said lord and reverend Archbishop for many years shouldered the task and office of the Inquisitor General against heretical pravity in all the realms of the Catholic Kings. And he converted to the Christian faith all the Moors in the city of Granada and baptized many with his own hands. And he was instrumental in the conversion to Christianity of all the Moors of the realm of Granada. They were countless in number, for the city was then very populous and had many inhabitants. And the same goes for the whole realm. And that was in the year 1497. And a little later all the Moors in the realm of Castile converted to Christianity, and that was in the year of Our Lord, 1502.

Furthermore, [Cisneros] had such fervour and zeal for the faith that he decided to expose his life to the danger of death and risk everything he had. And he set in train an expedition for the regions of the infidels in Africa to gain as much territory as he could and to subject the infidels to the holy Catholic faith. And he brought together as many troops as he could, both cavalry and peasants as footsoldiers, and went to the port of Cartajena, for he thought that this port was most convenient to advance his good project. And he embarked on 18 May in the year of the Lord 1509. And Our Lord gave him such good fortune and victory that by divine dispensation and benevolence he took in combat the city of Oran on the following Friday, which was the day after the Lord's Ascension. More than eight thousand Moors were taken captive and more than four thousand killed. And the booty taken there, according to the report of those present, was worth more than fifteen [my correction of "five hundred"] thousand ducats. Over three hundred Christian captives were freed, who had been held in the city's dungeon. And shortly afterwards he turned all mosques into churches and consecrated them.

Furthermore, in the year of the Lord 1516, on the day of St. Alfonso, which is 23 January, the most excellent and powerful Catholic King Don Fernando of illustrious memory passed away. And this happened in a place called Madrigalejo, a village in Trugillo, which is between Guadalupe and Medellin. And his body was taken to the city of Granada to be buried by the side of his wife, the said Queen Doña Ysabel, for he had given orders to be buried there. And before God took him from this life, he made the said Archbishop Governor General of the realms of Castile and Aragon, for his only daughter and heiress of Castile, called Doña Juana, the wife of King Don Filipe of illustrious memory, lived at that time a retired life at Tordesilla. On account of a certain impediment she could not be entrusted with the government. And with the consent of the grandees whom he was able to assemble there, [Cisneros], as stated, became governor. And he ruled these realms in great peace and concord and justice. And he greatly favoured the common people and was popular, both among the dependents of his archbishopric and all the realms which he had under his rule. And the Archbishop governed these realms from the death of King Don Filipe [1506] until King Don Fernando came from Italy, and after the death of King Don Fernando [1516] until the arrival of his grandson and Emperor Don Carlos, son of the said Señora Doña Juana and King Filipe. Thus, from the time when he was ordained Archbishop until his demise he lived twenty-two years and one month in a most praiseworthy manner, holding these offices and positions of honour.

Furthermore the lord and Archbishop, returning from the conquest of Oran, which was a great and memorable undertaking, did many other notable things both in the Cathedral of Toledo and in the whole of his see. He favoured especially and had much zeal for the study of divinity. He built at his own cost an imposing and sumptuous college in Alcala de Henares in which lectures are given in all the liberal arts and in canon law and theology, in Greek, Hebrew and medicine, by as many great doctors as he was able to bring together. And he gave to the college great income and permanent rents and grants and obtained for it many prebends and livings and was much involved in regulating and arranging all of those things. Thus many are graduating from the college and have graduated who are great men of learning, and there is no longer any need to go to other academies or colleges outside the realm. And the first year in which they began lectures in the disciplines was the year of the Lord 1508, on the day of Santiago, on which the students walked in procession from the college to the church, called Santiago, and there were then about five hundred students. And every day the number of teachers and students grew, and today the university is established and will be everlasting.

Also, he built beside the college in Alcala a monastery which is called Sant Juan de la Penitencia. It is meant for nuns and young women, so that those who want to take vows may stay there, and those who intend to marry may be helped with their marriage plans.

He also built at his cost a monastery in Toledo that is also called San Juan de la Penitencia, in the same form and manner as the one at Alcala. And to both he gave endowments and rents which were quite sufficient for the maintenance of those who lived there as well as for assisting with the marriages of those who wanted to be married.

He built another monastery in the village of Yllescas for nuns, and there too he left rents for their maintenance. He also built the Church of St. Iuste in Alcala and attached to it 17 canonries and 12 prebends. And the canons were professors of holy theology of the graduates in the said college, and if one canonry should become vacant it would be taken over by the oldest one in the college, who would then also be professor of theology. And the canonries were worth fifty thousand maravedis and the prebends fifteen thousand. Furthermore he stored in Toledo twenty thousand *fanegas* [a measure of 55 litres] of wheat in the granary of the said city that the city might have provisions in times of need and famine, and that the price of bread would not rise. He did this out of love for the poor. And all this he did at his own cost. Likewise he stored in the village of Alcala de Henares ten thousand *fanegas* of wheat. And in this village of Torrelaguna, in which he was born, he stored five thousand *fanegas*.

Finally, considering that God had bestowed on him such positions of honour and shown him such grace and given him possessions in this world for the purpose of doing good, and since he had benefited other places, there was no reason why his birthplace should be left without any benefit, a place where he had been born and spent his childhood. He therefore decided to show his benevolence by building at his cost there in Torrelaguna, which was his native village, that sumptuous and regal monastery and marvellous choir of the observant order of the glorious and seraphic father of ours, St. Francis. It is, from first to last, built of stone. And for the sake of vocations, he instituted the said monastery which is called La Madre de Dios. And he donated all the necessary furnishings, both for the church and for saying mass at the altars and the equipment of the sacristy, although not so grand as he had wished, for death overtook him. And he supplied all the other things which were necessary for the offices within the house. And he piped water to the house which cost him a quantity of maravedis. And the first year in which he began to build the said monastery was at the beginning of June of the year of the Lord 1510. And since Our Lord wanted to give him his reward and recognition for his work and good deeds, he took him from this present life in a place which is called Roa, in the county of Sirvela, at the time when he still had the government of the said realms. It happened on 8 November, the week after All Saints, in the year of the Lord 1517, and his body was taken for burial to the collegiate church of Alcala which he built for the honour and glory of Our Lord Jesus Christ and Saint Alfonso.

In addition to the aforesaid actions of the reverend prelate and cardinal, there were others worthwhile reporting, to be remembered and to serve as a model for future generations:

Firstly, that being the Guardian of Castañar, he was fervent in his faith and the desire to become a martyr, and the spirit gave him strength, and he took the path toward shedding his blood for Christ, but he was held back by God so that he could serve him in another way.

Secondly, he never departed from the rules governing the life of an observant monk in his manner of dress or sleeping arrangements, in spite of the rank of dignity and office to which God raised him.

Also, after he had been made archbishop and until his death he never allowed at his table idle or profane talk; and he always engaged in learned disputations in the various disciplines, especially theology. And because this was known, there were always famous scholars at his table who had come to participate in the disputations.

Also: He built in the Cathedral of Toledo the Mozarabic chapel and had the mass celebrated according to the Mozarabic rite, which is the oldest rite in the Latin church and differs from the Roman church, but with its authorization.

Also: He took great care to find scholars proficient in the various languages to translate the whole [Bible]. They had to have knowledge in Latin, Hebrew, Greek, and Chaldean.

Also: He instituted reform in the divine office in the See of Toledo, which was much corrupted both as far as the words and the singing was concerned.

Also: He printed diverse books that contained much learning but were little known, for the public benefit, and he made financial provisions for printing them all, because of his lasting love of learning.

Index